Best Plays of
Albert Innaurato

with an Introduction
by the author

Best Plays of
Albert Innaurato

with an Introduction
by the author

Coming of Age in Soho

Gemini

The Transfiguration of Benno Blimpie

Gay Presses of New York
1987

LIBRARY OF CONGRESS CATALOGING IN PUBLICATION DATA

Innaurato, Albert, 1948-
 Best Plays of Albert Innaurato.

  Contents: *Coming of Age in Soho—Gemini—
  The Transfiguration of Benno Blimpie*

  I. Title
  PS3559.N46A6 1987   812'.54   87-17668
  ISBN: 0-914017-14-4

Gay Presses of New York
Box 294, Village Station
New York, New York 10014

To Joe & Gail

Contents

Introduction by Albert Innaurato

INTRODUCTION BY ALBERT INNAURATO

Two of the plays included here are early plays of mine, though not the earliest. Of the three, *Benno Blimpie* came first. I wrote it while I was a student at the Yale School of Drama. It was begun my first year there, 1972, and finished later that summer, while I was staying at Edward Albee's house for writers (sometimes called The Stable by cynics). Christopher Durang was also at The Stable and a fellow student at Yale during this time. We had long talks about the future of American Dramaturgy not realizing that we would eventually make much of our money writing for television (and he, later, appearing on television). Mr. Albee we glimpsed only at a distance that summer. But it strikes me as curious now that two young writers hatched their first distinctive plays in a house owned by the last American playwright to make a great dent in the awareness of the larger American public. Though Mr. Albee has not had much commercial success over the past decade and has been the victim of an especially vicious press in that time, he still remains far better known in name and work than any of us who have come along since, and I am not forgetting Messrs. Shepard and Mamet. For a very large public their work, as well as that of Durang and myself, has about it something elusive. All these writers are produced far more often in small rather than large theaters, by young, *avant garde* companies rather than established regional theaters, and none has had a conventional success on Broadway. Mamet and Innaurato have come closest. Mamet's fine play *Glengarry Glen Ross* won a Pulitzer Prize and had a short, not very profitable run. My play, *Gemini,* ran for more than four years but was roundly despised by the Powers On Broadway, and was never nominated for any awards.

It seems to me that Albee is the last living American playwright to see a string of his plays produced on Broadway (aside from the very different Neil Simon), to have reasonable to very successful runs there and to be accounted a figure to be taken seriously in American letters. The younger writers who have made brief splashes since remain essentially coterie writers with larger or smaller followings depending on just how much *The New York Times* is panting about them. When PEN, the American society of writers, gave a vast, highly publicized international conference in New York City, Albee and the much older Arthur Miller (who has in fact written fewer plays of unequivocal value) were the only playwrights included, and

Miller the only active participant. This seemed to me one of many signs that most American literati, rightly or wrongly, regretfully or not, have written off the American Theater, as indeed have many quondam participants in that theater. I am amused by the strident denials I read of this, only to be confounded anew by the suffocating proof of it, which grows more overwhelming every season.

As for writing *Benno,* it began as a very vivid dream in which the events seemed frighteningly real. Solving the dream in play form was difficult, to say the least, and I suppose one can legitimately criticize the play for combining—uneasily—elements of naturalism and surrealism.

I planned *Gemini* in New York while I had a Guggenheim grant. But the grant ran out and I had to get a series of temporary jobs, mostly humiliating ones. Then, disaster struck; an old medical condition which had been operated on at Yale acted up, or more accurately, the surgical procedure, which had been experimental, came undone and I started to hemorrhage. I had no health insurance. I developed a fever, lost my job as a messenger and had to go begging for assistance. It was the worst period of my life, and I wrote *Gemini*—perhaps as much a demonstration of my own will to survive as to escape the crisis. Eventually, and not for the last time, Howard Stein (who had been Dean of Students at Yale), came to my rescue and saw that another operation was made possible. This was a painful and frightening procedure, complicated when the surgical wound became infected causing a high fever. When the fever broke I left the hospital, creating considerable hysteria among the interns and nurses at Yale New Haven Hospital. I wanted to die. That's when I wrote the last scene of *Gemini;* the next morning, the wound stopped oozing, and the swelling decidedly lessened. Bad writers, I'm sorry to admit, often give their writing mystical significance, but those who told me that the play had a 'healing' quality may have been on to something. I polished the script under a Rockefeller grant which arrived too late to help my health but provided some comfort.

escape the crisis. Eventually, and not for the last time, Howard Stein (who had been Dean of Students at Yale), came to my rescue and saw that another operation was made possible. This was a painful and frightening procedure, complicated when the surgical wound became infected causing a high fever. When the fever broke I left the hospital, creating considerable hysteria among the interns and nurses at Yale New Haven Hospital. I wanted to die. That's when I wrote the last scene of *Gemini;* the next morning, the wound stopped oozing, and the swelling decidedly lessened. Bad writers, I'm sorry to admit, often give their writing mystical significance, but those who told me that the play had a 'healing' quality may have been on to something. I polished the script under a Rockefeller grant which arrived too late to help my health but provided some comfort.

I derived enormous pleasure from writing *Gemini.* It was not much liked when it first began to circulate in manuscript—whether this was due to my erratic typing, shortsightedness on the part of those early readers, or legitimate critical concerns, I can't say. *Gemini,* during its long run, was probably rightly considered a "back door" success. It snuck up on the New York Theater and embarrassed the mocking opinion makers who had damned it early on. Of course, they punished it and its writer for years afterwards. It became the play that refused to die.

I'm almost tempted into nostalgia remembering how *Gemini* came to be produced; I'm convinced it was a time such as we'll not see again in the American Theater: the era of off-off-Broadway, the last time New York had a living theater, albeit a theater of poverty, and in the wake of this, a community of theater artists, working together.

Peter Schifter, who wanted to direct the play, actively lobbied Bob Moss (who then ran Playwrights Horizons) to give it a production. Moss was resistant, he kept saying *Gemini* wasn't "gay" enough for him. (That would have surprised Ross Wetzsteon, then evidently doing graduate work with Rex Reed; for some years later in the *Village Voice,* Wetzsteon would coin the word "gayest" to describe my work and that of Christopher Durang, with *Gemini* the main culprit.) Schifter, that spring, directed *Benno Blimpie* at the now defunct Direct Theatre. Mel Gussow gave the play a good review which began a change in Moss' mind. That fall, Andre Bishop, about to replace Moss, agreed with Schifter and a production was scheduled. Our budget was about five hundred dollars for everything (nowadays, in the same theater, a conservative budget would be eight to ten times as much.) As usual in those circumstances getting the play on unembarrassingly was a matter of happenstance, luck and favors given. Luckily, at this time, a community of actors living in New York were excited by the notion of working on new plays and were willing to support themselves however they could to act on stage. Of course, the realities of living on rather little money in Manhattan were less grim than they've become, and there was still the conviction that any day Broadway would revive and rescue us all. Sigourney Weaver, who Schifter and I had known at Yale, agreed to play Judith and broght along a good friend of hers, Reed Birney, to play Randy. Anne de Salvo, who had played the mother, and Jon Polito who had played Benno in that earlier production of *Benno Blimpie* played Francis and Lucille. Jonathan Hadary who had read Herschel fabulously in the play's first reading in the living room of Mike Tucker and Jill Eikenberry (a reading Danny DeVito attended with two lush beauties on his arm) did Herschel. We cast Bruce Weitz who I knew through Eikenberry, as the father and couldn't find a Bunny. Everyone we handed a script thought the woman impossibly vulgar. Though this was 1977, actors were uneasy about saying 'fuck'. (This reminds me of a story about the casting of the off-Broadway production of *Benno*. Bobby Drivas and Jimmy Coco had persuaded that Andalusian charmer and fabulist with a soft spot for nuns, Adela Holtzer, to produce the play. Having rejected the brilliant de Salvo as too young, Drivas and Coco couldn't cast the mother. The script went to every major actress over forty in New York, and was promptly returned, usually with unflattering remarks about the author. One tough lady decided to return the script in person. She arrived at Holtzer's office without an appointment. As she was very distinguished, they let her in. She strode into Adela's inner sanctum. Adela was delighted, surely Miss_____ had come to accept that wonderful part. "You fucking spic cunt!" screamed the actress. Adela stiffened in incipient rage: "How dare you," she cried in her accent, "I am no spic, I born Spanish." "You fucking Spanish cunt," screamed the actress in her famous voice which had thrilled millions in a dozen toilet bowl commercials. "I am a professional in this business and you send me this piece of shit and expect me to say those awful words? Well, fuck you!" She hurled the script right at Adela's head and strode out of the office, pushing Adela's factotum of the time, a very large man, to the floor. Luckily, I was thin in those days and had been able to look insignificant and occupied in a corner.

Meanwhile, ironically at the same time, Schifter was going crazy trying to find a Bunny. Finally he called me and said, "I found one. I am sending her over." Jessica James, a well-traveled former showgirl, strode in, wearing tight jeans stretched over a voluptuous figure. There was a Chemex pot of cold coffee on the floor of my basement apartment on Waverly Place, and she gulped it down, striding nervously around the room. Then, without warning, she launched into Bunny's wildest speech, which she had more or less memorized (then and later she used the rule, when in doubt add a fuck). I thought anyone able to gulp cold day-old coffee like that deserved the part. And so the play was cast. There were problems of course—but relatively few. These actors still believed in theater and wanted to act on the stage. They were amazingly dedicated. They rehearsed in an unheated condemned building on Times Square in what was to be the coldest November in New York history. They put up with an inexperienced author and director. They were excited to be working on a new play, and all would have thought long and hard about leaving the project. Weitz did leave to go to L.A. (he ended up one of the stars of *Hill Street Blues*). I don't blame him. He was young for the father but old enough to be anxious about making a living, he had recently married and I'm sure suspected even if the play was some kind of success against enormous odds he would hardly benefit from it. It was a sign of the times that he felt terribly guilty and the other actors judged him severely. But after all, we were all working for free—the most we could expect was to split the box office take for the final week. (It came to about twenty dollars each.) Since then, I've seen actors blithely walk out of Broadway, off-Broadway and very prominent institutional theater productions where there were real if modest salaries with nary a backward glance—their colleagues more envious than censorious. What was astounding about this first cast was their belief in the play. They wept and laughed through it, and worked unstintingly hard to make every moment live. The actor with whom we replaced Weitz, Tom Mardiosian, learned a huge part in forty-eight hours and leapt right in. They all believed the play had a destiny; and when everyone else mocked them, sometimes angrily, they shrugged. They simply knew better. Careers embitter all of us, I guess. Hell, life embitters all of us, it becomes too difficult to believe the best of people. But for those months, these actors willed their love of the piece and the associations to that love into three dimensions; and I think as much as anything, what moved and thrilled the early audiences of *Gemini* was encountering a radiance on stage many had forgotten can exist in the real world.

We played the appointed three week run at Playwrights Horizons. The reviews were very good, especially Gussow's in the *Times*. We had some hope of transferring to an institutional theater but they all backed off. We asked Marshall Mason and members of his company at the then prestigious Circle Rep to come see the play (they had already lost the script which in the early days had been sent to them only to be misplaced by then literary manager, Danny Somebody.) No commercial producer would come see the play with an eye toward moving it. When Helen Merrill, the agent for the play, tried to interest people, they laughed at her. The subject matter (I suppose they meant that the play's openness about homosexuality and the lack of condemnation) or the language, or both, were sure proof that the play would sink commercially. It looked as though we would close.

Then, three days before the last performance, Jay Broad called Bob Moss. Broad ran a theater in Huntington, Long Island called PAF; it was a regional theater run with the novel notion that only new American plays about American people should be presented to living American audiences. He had lost a play which was to go into the January slot, and it was too late to find another. He had read the *Times'* review about this weird play by an Armenian fag and while he thought the subject matter might be too much, the review said the play was well directed. "He's an Italian," said Bob Moss, "And I don't care much for the play, but it certainly is well directed and acted and might just be what you need." Broad came with his staff to the next to the last performance. He hated the play. They loved it. He didn't want to do it. They persuaded him it was ideal since the Huntington audience consisted of many Italian-Americans from a working-class background. The day after the last performance at PH contracts were signed for PAF.

Changes had to be made—several cast members had gotten offers during its run. But we added still more actors who came to believe as passionately in the play's destiny as their predecessors. These included Bob Picardo to play Francis and Danny Aiello as Fran. I rewrote the play in the time between these productions, cheered on by Reed Birney, who had a conviction, like the earliest Christians, that there would be life after PAF.

One change that was widely misreported and usually held against me over the next few years was the ending. In the original script (on file at the Library of the Performing Arts in New York), Judith, in act one, spews some Dante, then leaps out of the second floor window into the trash cans below. She tells Francis that she made the "great leap" and was uninjured, meaning that to resolve his sexuality all he needs to do is declare himself unambiguously. At the end of the play,

Judith and Randy leave, walking down the alley. At the least second, Francis leaps out of the second storey window into the trash cans. They come running back. That was it. The first night at PH, the stage manager made a mistake and called the final blackout just as Francis jumped, leading those present to believe he'd tried to commit suicide. After that performance, those in power at PH lobbied for either a "gay ending" or an unearned sad one, where Francis sat in his window alone and smoked, listening to his Callas records. That was, perforce, the one I chose. At PAF I took the opportunity to expand the original ending, making it easier to stage (the actors, rightly, were afraid that all that jumping out the window was dangerous), and including the family characters. But the spirit of the ending is the same. Francis decides to go to Boston, a more sensible choice than sitting alone in his room, hiding, with only canned Callas for company. The play doesn't definitively answer the question of Francis' sexuality. He may go on to be an exclusive homosexual, a bisexual (I believe in bisexuality, finding it neither a fiction nor a cop out), or perhaps (least likely) a typical heterosexual. I've always been puzzled by objections to this ending. I wonder, did Kinsey live and die in vain? His studies and my own observations and I believe those of anyone objective is that sexuality in humans is mysterious, various and changeable. I'm afraid I think that in a world where there need be no anxiety about the birth rate or the survival of infants, that love, or for that matter sexual ecstasy, have about the same value no matter the genitals of the participants—and that only rape is criminal and to be punished. In my opinion the horror and tragedy of AIDS as contradicting this for I am not talking about specific sexual acts and certainly not promiscuity; I am talking about the exchange of feelings not the exchange of fluids.

This is what I intended to convey by Francis' choice: life is more than labels, and more than merely being accepted by others. The effort must be made to live freely, without a safety net and that is what he sets out to do in the end, period. And those who think of me as a misogynist writer might ponder that a woman teaches Francis this.

To continue the saga of *Gemini*, we opened at PAF in a terrible snowstorm, for an audience (beside the reviewers) of thirty or so people. But the play caught on. For the first and last time in my life to date I had the feeling of power that playwrights must have known historically. Since they did only new plays, PAF had a meet-the-playwright-evening once a week. One simply *had* to attend. I was told not to expect more than a handful of people to stay; warned that they were likely to be those offended by the play. The first night we were scheduled for this, the entire audience stayed. And when Broad introduced me, they gave me an ovation such as I never have gotten since. I was amazed that my play, which I had gotten used to being defensive about—didn't many of the New York trendies think it silly, coarse, false?—could move these people so much.

I'm not making great claims for *Gemini* as "art"—there are better, greater, profounder plays, of course. But all the same there was a genuine electricity about *Gemini* in those days that I am proud of.

Gemini was extended at PAF and again we all worked to get producers interested in moving it back into the city. No dice. We got to the last week of our run and faced the fact that we would close and that would be it for the play. No one had come forth with an offer to publish it, nor did it seem the kind of script which would do well in the regionals or sell to the movies.

Three days before our last performance I was standing in the Chemical Bank on Sheridan Square in the Village. As usual, it had just been robbed and several dozen unfortunate customers were standing in line waiting for a delivery of money so we could cash checks. The usual security guard was playing his banjo, singing, and trying to cadge money out of the restive Villagers standing in line. My favorite teller (the one who had been robbed) was having a hysterical fit behind the counter; the robber, in his note, had called her a fat pig, and she had just spent several thousand dollars on the Protein-Sparing Fast. As usual, we New Yorkers were keeping our eyes averted as much as possible, just hoping the money delivery truck wouldn't be held up as well. But peripherally, I saw a tall, spindly man with long hair who looked familiar. He seemed to be eyeing me, screwing up his face as though trying to place me. Suddenly I recognized him; it was Marshall Mason. Nerving myself up and resigned to losing my place in line, I approached him. "Hello, Mr. Mason," I said, "I'm sure you don't remember me, but I'm the playwright with the long name and you saw my play *Gemini*, a few months ago at Playwrights Horizons." "So, that's who you are," he cried. "Yes," I continued, "I know you didn't care that much for the play in that version, but, you know, we've been playing out at PAF and I've rewritten it and it's quite successful, maybe you..." He grabbed my arm. "You mean, it's still playing? Right now, near New York? Oh my God, honey, we've just lost Julie Bovasso's play and we desperately need something to do in two weeks. We've been trying to get *Shadow Box*, now that's a great play, but they're greedy, they want to bring it to Broadway, and while your play wasn't very good, it may be the best we can do. Is there some way Lance and Jerry Arrow and I can go see it?" "Oh yes," I said, inwardly blessing the bank robber who had made this meeting possible, "I'll arrange it."

That night, Marshall, Lanford Wilson, and Jerry Arrow went to see the play at PAF, and the next day they were in negotiation with Helen Merrill. We went into rehearsals for two weeks, previewed, then opened. With a synchronicity which only happens in 'B' movies, *Benno Blimpie,* produced by Adela Holtzer, opened the night before *Gemini,* and Albert Innaurato got his half hour in the sun. I won't underestimate the value of the Circle Rep engagement. Though many of their company actively disliked the play, its' author and several of his cast members, our successful run there and our encountering Jerry Arrow, then their business manager, made the eventual move to Broadway possible; Arrow's never-say-die attitude, learned from years in the institutional theater, as well as his willingness to risk everything, led to the long run on Broadway.

Perhaps this is enough about "the making of *Gemini.*" The saga doesn't stop here, believe me, but I think you get the idea. The long run was facilitated by a vulgar television commercial which did indeed sell the play to a particular audience but misrepresented it. Some avoided the play because they felt confident the commercial told the whole story. Did it? I don't think so. Are the characters grotesques? I don't think that, either. Their behavior is less extreme than what we see reported every day in the milder news broadcasts. But even where they are outrageous by the strictest standards of middle class decorum, there is, I believe, suffering, dignity and love within them. I think the final way I'd like to describe *Gemini* is a tiny prayer that good will will win out, that one may find a home to come back to, that friends will welcome one always and that one's craziest neighbor—irritating and gross occasionally—may in some secret way be a creature of beauty and wisdom.

In our society success is widely accounted to be the answer to all problems. After *Gemini,* and *Benno Blimpie,* my problems increased. I lived the cliche of the American writer's life: my successes—for what they were worth—gave others the right to untrammeled and irresponsible viciousness. Thus, a few months after *Gemini* reached Broadway (I was 30 at the time), I read Richard Eder's declaration in *The New York Times* that my "promise was broken." Even on the fact of it this was a ridiculous assertion. What? My promise broken? Really? At thirty? Having written two widely if not universally hailed plays and several others considered at least interesting? The cause of this attack was a play of mine called *Ulysses in Traction*. Eder's review wasn't simply a professional bad review, trying to take into account all the factors that can contribute to a disappointing evening in the theater—including the playwright's failure to solve his play—it was a personal attack. The playwright had extolled a gay character while daring to refer to "heterosexual impotence." While in fact, the gay character is the one who is impotent. I felt what Edward Albee must have felt throughout much of his career. What was really being reviewed was what the reviewer *thought* to be my private life. (Like Wetzsteon, Eder on this and other occasions wrote as "fag basher".) The secret agenda of his review was that good potent heterosexuals (like him) must keep the queers down, for if they aren't kept down they'll take over. Although *Ulysses in Traction* was no more than a journeyman work in comparison, I understood what Albee must have felt when his masterpiece, *Who's Afraid of Virginia Woolf* was attacked in similar terms. In this case, the fag bashing scuttlebutt was that Albee knew nothing about heterosexuals and had based his play on the amorous intrigues of four men. Ironically, this "criticism" was spread, and I think invented, by a "critic" who's own marriage resembled that of George and Martha's, without the love. These sallies were usually unjust but it is hard not to internalize them, and they prove irresistible, especially to lesser arts journalists who can't resist flirting with libel. I was not Eder's only target and it isn't a comfort that he didn't last long at the *Times,* in fact his tenure there as a theater reviewer may have been the shortest in history. Recently the *Times* has tried to be fair in covering homosexual's plays and the current reviewers are not blatantly sexist. But one can continue to find this sort of thing in other places, even surprising ones like the *Village Voice.* Had I not been the target of his earlier sexist attacks and near libel, I'd have been amused by Wetzsteon's turnaround in trying to outdo Liz Smith and Rex Reed in smarmy praise of *Torch Song Trilogy.* (Is this reverse sexism, as the play extolls gay monogamy?) There is something disgusting in such opportunism. Wetzsteon, presumably always a step behind, had caught on that "gay" was chic and leapt onto that bandwagon. I wonder, now that there is a backlash in this country, if we can expect a renewed series of attacks on those suspected or known to be homosexuals from him or his minions at the *Voice*. Fervent opportunists are worse than flagrant bigots; for one thing they are usually more unprincipled; they may not build the Concentration Camps—they justify them.

In 1985, in *New York Magazine,* John Simon, reviewing a non-gay play, accused the playwright of having a "faggot sense of humor," thus capping a career based on pandering to pseudo-intellectual homophobia. Despite numerous letters of protest, not only did he retain his hatcheting job, he was given a flattering cover story by the gay publication, *The New York Native*. Letters written to *New York Magazine* after that review (it wasn't of my play), started out by saying: "We normally agree with John Simon. . . " But how do they know? Judging from virtually non-existent runs, they rarely see the plays he praises, never the ones he pans, how can they "agree"? Other published objections were to the contemptuous associations of the term he'd used. But few dared to question Simon's basic assumptions. In my opinion, only the most unlettered philistine assumes, as Simon and his adherents like Wetzsteon all too evidently do, that a talented writer's quotidian sexual orientation colors his or her writing. And only the most ignorant bigot assumes that a homosexual knows nothing about or is always hostile towards heterosexuality. Homosexuals are products of heterosexuality, are raised by heterosexuals, are surrounded by them their entire lives, and often enough have (because they want to) heterosexual experiences. A perceptive and talented homosexual writer would have to be deaf, dumb, blind, and seriously benighted to write inaccurately about heterosexuality, or as stupid, dishonest and bigoted as many of our theater reviewers. I write this not out of pique but because it is becoming clear that there is a well funded and powerful element in our society which has targeted homosexuals as scapegoats, presumably to distract the middle class from a still troubled economy, widespread poverty, growing illiteracy, and a frightening moral decay which has nothing whatever to do with sexual preference but with a large population who sincerely believe their lives are hopeless and meaningless and who gallop to procure surcease in any substance for sale on the streets. Recently, the Vatican has spewed disgusting bigotry and inhumanity about homosexuals, using AIDS as an excuse. The Supreme Court found homosexuals not protected by the Constitution and the Chief Justice at the time, Mr. Burger, displayed huge ignorance by taking the nonsense of the television evangelists as fact, whereas the history of homosexuals and their acceptance is far more complicated. Even a small mindless gesture like Simon's needs to be challenged, for it is precisely this kind of scurrilous agitprop which leads to censorship and sexual repression.

Returning to my own private misfortunes brings us to *Coming of Age in Soho*. In 1983, fearing that I had lost my gift I wrote a play quickly for Playwright's Horizons and called it *Herself as Lust*. It never opened. I felt even more of a failure after this. But the idea wouldn't leave me alone. I expanded the play, changed many details and called it *Coming of Age in Soho*. I directed a workshop version in Seattle where the play ran five hours. I did some cutting and did a reading for Joe Papp and his wife, Gail Merrifield. Joe decided to produce it the following Fall.

We went into rehearsal optimistically but had trouble from the first. The central role, a woman composer named Gioconda, was huge and seemed to require a mixture of Anna Magnani and Cher with a touch of Meryl Streep thrown in. Several ladies with some of those qualities were either not interested or unavailable. The reputable actress we cast was wrong for the role, which became an enormous obstacle for her. She left, and her replacement, a good egg with a lot of comedic talent, couldn't rise to the more emotional moments or really suggest an irresistible sex object—for the plot of the play turned on the fight over Gioconda between the well-heeled and genteel Mafia lawyer who had kept her in her early years, and a runaway prep-schooler who she lets stay in her loft. Meanwhile, the play's length continued to be a problem. Cutting seemed to disrupt the densely woven texture of the play, scattering rather than refocusing it. We had the usual problems with some other actors— Networks stealing our first leading man, a prestigious workshop stealing our first Pasquale. After a few previews and some mad rewriting it looked like a disaster.

Joe Papp decided to rescue me. He suggested I write a new play retaining some elements of the old one but replacing Gioconda with a man based on Bartholemew Dante, called Beatrice by everyone, a character already important in the play as a supporting character. Papp felt the actor playing Beatrice, John Procaccino, seemed better than any of the actresses we had seen—or at least more at ease in the Innaurato style. He also felt that reorganizing the play around a figure rather like myself might force me to find a way to focus the play more truly. And finally, he felt that the theme of one man's attempt to define his sexuality might be more timely and electrifying for an audience than the more conventional theme of a woman divided between her art, her lovers (one much younger) and her child. He gave me nine days to do it; we recast as needed, rehearsed for two weeks, previewed for two more weeks, then opened for the New York critics.

This *Coming of Age in Soho* became in fact something quite different from the old play of the same title, more a new work than a radical rewrite. This text is more personal, which disturbed some reviewers. This play is more autobiographical than any I've written, though precisely how I'd rather leave a mystery: I have never been able to reconcile fantasy with reality. I'm not insane, I understand that actions have consequences and the older one gets the more one pays for one's irresponsibility, but I can't help myself. In the character of Beatrice, I confronted some of my fantasies and their consequences.

In reading this edition, the first time the entire text has been published and will be seen by anyone not involved at the Public Theater (for good and bad reasons quite a lot was cut in the first previews) I was moved, and I hope others will be moved too by Beatrice's journey from aged child to grown man. He faces some of his fantasies made flesh—a life on his own, an adolescent who loves him—and has to face up to the real-life implications of those things. He learns the difference between pursuing "objects" with intense fivolity, and reaching out to real people. For the first time in his life he tries to balance the equation of desire and duty, where the future of all those involved are crucial elements. With difficulty, he accepts being the age he is, no longer a demi-man bound in perpetual adolescence, but an adult trying to seize the fleeting present, capable of learning from his past.

Beatrice is a man with a harmless bondage fantasy, and bondage becomes a metaphor in the play for his inertia and paralysis. One action in the play is for him to "free" or untie himself; another is for him to "free" his sexual object, risking rejection or, in the case of *Coming of Age in Soho,* renunciation.

Beatrice is really in love with Dy, and their love scene is as I think of it now, the first I have ever written. It has little to do with sexual desire, manipulation or role playing, nor is one party kind and the other obsessed. They love each other as equals, and in denying himself, Beatrice finds for the first time in his life the pleasure or pain of love untethered to questions of gender, role playing, or futurity. Also in the play is the question of parenthood. Puer is both a real person and a part of Beatrice's process of growing up. As a man who fundamentally hates himself, who can deal with himself only by preserving the fantasy of perpetual adolescence, Beatrice must reject his son; fear, mystification masquerading as dislike. Beatrice doesn't learn to "love" his son in a trice, at the end of the play; he may never have the sort of paternal feelings many people (straight and gay) have when they produce children. But by accepting Puer and Puer's love, Beatrice can begin to accept himself, and it is the hope of the play that this new acceptance will untie Beatrice the writer, allowing him to be productive, that impossibly genuine thing, "an artist."

It strikes me now as curious that I've never been able to manage a conventionally simple ending. I may be incapable of hope. Though part of it is, that in *Gemini* and *Coming of Age*, I became so involved with these characters (they were realer to me than I am to myself) that the endings reflect an unwillingness to let go, to settle their fates once and for all. Quantum mechanics suggests to us something like infinite probabilities—every situation has many outcomes and all of them may happen, even if we with our limited consciousness must for sanity's sake acknowledge only one, in three dimensions. Maybe in *Gemini* and *Coming of Age* I've tried with my limited skill to suggest infinite endings. *Benno* is the most desolate of these plays.

If I may end on an autobiographical note, my life has turned into an attempt to escape what at one time seemed my inevitable end. I'm not sure I have escaped, but I am grateful to The Gay Presses of New York for publishing these plays, and that little gesture of faith may be part of my survival.

—*New York*
December 1986

Coming of Age in Soho

Coming of Age in Soho

Dramatis Personae

Bartholomew Dante—("Beatrice")
Patricia Foscari Dante—his wife
Odysseus MacDowell—("Dy"), sixteen years old
Puer Dante—Beatrice's son, thirteen years old
Danny Amato—eighteen years old, entry level position in the Mafia
Pasquale Foscari—his boss, Patricia's brother
Trajan MacDowell—nineteen years old, Dy's brother

Scene
Beatrice's new loft in Soho, New York City, around 1985.

ACT ONE

[*The loft of* BARTHOLEMEW DANTE, *in Soho.* BARTHOLEMEW—
called BEATRICE *by friends and others—has just moved in. The
loft is bare. There are boxes scattered about, perhaps a table or
two. As a result the room seems enormous: there are doors to
a bathroom, and a small inner room. The windows, huge and
as yet unbarred, command a startling view of the Manhattan
skyline; it is about to rain.* BEATRICE *is an Italian-American
man of thirty-six. There is something attractive about him but
it is hard to say what exactly. Certainly he is not good looking
in a conventional way: he is poised on the brink of what may
become a decidedly chubby middle age. Despite his nickname*
BEATRICE *seems conventionally masculine in manner.* BEATRICE
*is looking edgy and irritated. After a moment, a blond young
man—perhaps twenty—enters from the adjoining room. He is
having some trouble moving since he is tied to a chair. He is
dressed in jeans but is barefoot and barechested. Coyly, he has
popped the first button of the jeans open. He looks eager but
puzzled.*]

ARNOLD: [*Hopefully, to* BEATRICE] I've tied myself to this chair—
aren't you coming?

BEATRICE: [*Embarrassed*] Look ... [*Doesn't know his name*]

ARNOLD: Arnold, sir.

BEATRICE: Look, Arnold, I'm just not into it. I'm sorry after you
went to all that trouble.

ARNOLD: Oh, like did I overachieve? I do that sometimes. I
should have waited for you to tie me up.

BEATRICE: I don't want to tie you up.

ARNOLD: In a different position?

BEATRICE: [*Meaning no*] Thanks.

ARNOLD: Gosh! How insensitive of me! I should have tied you
up!

[*Suddenly the outer door of the loft is thrust open.* PATRICIA
GIAMBATTISTA DANTE *stands in the doorway, surveying her
ex-husband standing over a youth tied to a chair.*]

PATRICIA: Oh Beatrice, still at it?!

[PATRICIA *is an attractive, smart and tough woman of thirty-*

*six. She is more amused than shocked at what she sees.
Standing behind her is* DANNY AMATO; *nineteen years old and
in an entry level position in the Mafia. Danny is carrying an
armchair,* PATRICIA *is carrying a tape deck and a box of
tapes.*]

BEATRICE: [*Not pleased*] Patricia, how did you get in?

PATRICIA: Bribed the super! [*To* DANNY] Put it anywhere!

DANNY: [*Entering*] Yo! Hi, Beatrice.

BEATRICE: Hi, Danny.

ARNOLD: [*Still tied to the chair*] Who's she?

PATRICIA: I'm the wife!

BEATRICE: [*Sharp*] Ex-wife!

PATRICIA: [*Serene*] Not absolutely ex yet. I know you wanted to
ditch all your possessions when you ditched me but I
thought you'd need a chair and miss your music so I brought
them. I also brought provisions—soup and tea, Beatrice.

ARNOLD: [*Vainly trying to put this together.*] Beatrice? Your wife
calls you Beatrice?

PATRICIA: His last name is Dante, his first initial is B so we call
him Beatrice for Dante.

ARNOLD: What?

DANNY: Beatrice for Dante, everybody knows that!

BEATRICE: [*To* PATRICIA, *aggrieved*] You could have called.

PATRICIA: You don't have a phone. Why don't you untie him?

DANNY: [*Eagerly*] Let me, it's part of my training. [*Starts untying*
ARNOLD]

ARNOLD: [*As* DANNY*unties him*] Hi, what's your name?

PATRICIA: Danny, why don't you go park the car?

DANNY: Yo! [*Leaves*]

ARNOLD: [*Both* PATRICIA *and* BEATRICE *are staring at him.*] I
think I can untie myself ... [*Still partially tied to the chair,
retreats into the inner room.*]

PATRICIA: [*Goodnaturedly but enjoying* BEATRICE's *discomfort.*]
Really, Beatrice, when are you going to grow up? You're too
old to be playing cowboys and Indians.

BEATRICE: He was in my literary techniques class last semester.

PATRICIA: What were you teaching him?

BEATRICE: Suspense. I was about to rip his jeans off.

PATRICIA: Is that why they fired you?

BEATRICE: They found somebody who needed the pittance less.

PATRICIA: And you know what my shrink says: This is all because you can't tolerate intimacy.

BEATRICE: On the contrary, bondage is a great icebreaker.

PATRICIA: Not the bondage, damn you—*leaving me!*

[ARNOLD *enters, fully dressed, in a trendy mixture of punk and preppy, slightly abashed, dignified.*]

ARNOLD: Good evening, Professor Dante, Mrs. Dante—thank you for the private lesson. [*Rushes out*]

[PATRICIA *makes herself at home, smiles sweetly.* BEATRICE *waits at the open door, expected her to leave.*]

PATRICIA: [*After a moment*] So you're still in your mood.

BEATRICE: Leaving you forever is scarcely a mood.

PATRICIA: [*Lighting a cigarette*] Well, I'm not going to beg you to return.

BEATRICE: Of course not. Bribe maybe; threaten if that doesn't work.

PATRICIA: You're the one into S & M.

BEATRICE: Bondage is not S & M; it's a combination of restraint, engineering and knotty problems. Besides, I couldn't do anything with him.

PATRICIA: The health crisis, huh?

BEATRICE: I didn't want to do anything with him.

PATRICIA: Maybe you're growing up.

BEATRICE: With him or anyone else.

PATRICIA: Oh, you're regressing.

BEATRICE: Will you ever stop thinking of the universe of human feelings as a tiny river bounded by the land of the trite on one side and the continent of the cliched on the other? Is it because you went to the University of Virginia Law School?

PATRICIA: Right up there with the Kennedys.

BEATRICE: Except you passed everything.

PATRICIA: With honors.

BEATRICE: Just think, from Tenth and Federal, South Philadelphia U.S. of A., I'm a failed novelist and you're the first Mafia Don with a cervix!

PATRICIA: What's all this Mafia shit? I'm on the legal end. Anyway I'm running for Congress like everybody else. Now look, cut the bullshit, I want you back. (BEATRICE *grimaces*] All right, I want a long series of explanations. We were together—on and off—for fourteen years. I kept you most of that time. I asked for very little. I didn't want a standard demanding hubby and you were—shall we say—disinclined to the domestic. Did I ever rein you in, inhibit you? Okay, so it wasn't the most spontaneous kind of love match, but it was a love match, a great arrangement. And please, stop grimacing like that. Look at this place, it's bare, like your life, like my life since you left. What the fuck are you doing?

BEATRICE: You are forcing me to be very un-Soho and commit cliche but here goes: I had to be free.

PATRICIA: You were free when I was keeping you.

BEATRICE: Free on a leash! And let's not exaggerate the number of years involved. How many times did I run away and live apart?

PATRICIA: You never filed for divorce and you always came back. There was a connection between us you honored no matter where you went or what pose you struck—but this—this severing...

BEATRICE: It was time to cut and bury the umbilical cord!

PATRICIA: Look at all you wrote with me; there were even some royalties. Your biggest success was with me...

BEATRICE: My cult classic which everyone thinks is a joke?

PATRICIA: And don't forget—I rescued you!

BEATRICE: This aria!

PATRICIA: Fifteen years ago you showed up at my door...

BEATRICE: [*Anticipating her*] Bleeding, friendless and broke...

PATRICIA: Without insurance, without hope. I paid. Do you remember what a wreck you were? You were fresh from shacking up with that German Terrorist...

BEATRICE: Now, we don't know for a fact that she was a terrorist—although that did look an awful lot like her with all the machine guns in Time Magazine...

PATRICIA: Look, face it, she was German and a Terrorist and as I recall a mother too—didn't she bear you a son?

BEATRICE: You are not making the case for yourself you think, even by bringing up Henrietta the Terrorist.

PATRICIA: And all these women! Doesn't that tell you something about yourself despite your constant claiming inversion? Not that I care if you're bisexual!

BEATRICE: I am not bisexual! I am a homosexual who suffers temporary amnesia in the presence of strong-willed ladies.

PATRICIA: But you've always been miserable in the fag world. You can never score, they think you're ugly, they think you're old—

BEATRICE: I don't think it says much for my heterosexuality that it results from rejection and cowardice; in any case failing hasn't stopped my longings, any more than it's stopped my writings. Look, Patricia, thanks for the armchair and the tapes—I did miss them. Let's stay friendly acquaintances who see each other once a year at Macy's and wave—okay?

PATRICIA: I don't buy any of this—

BEATRICE: What was the first thing I said to you?

PATRICIA: Help me.

BEATRICE: After that.

PATRICIA: I need five hundred a month to be comfortable.

BEATRICE: Doesn't your position strike you as strange? I was making myself your whore; you were a female john purchasing not beautiful potent youths but a quasi-intellectual wreck of a would-be artist. Talk about kinky! But in one of our early conversations I said to you, as I recall, that I thought in nature there were no such things as heterosexuals and homosexuals but only a complicated series of acts and the people who commit them. Oh for a while, I admit it, I enjoyed living as a heterosexual manque. But that was a lie.

BEATRICE: I'd run away from you, back into the gay world and be miserable there too—broke and lonely. Then I'd run back to you—at least I wouldn't be broke and lonely—but I'd be just as miserable. So, no, I didn't come here to be gay. I came here to try and center myself. Remember back in South Philly when you and I were just friends? How we'd sit and dream about New York, about the arts ... And you thought, everyone thought, I thought I had talent and should write. Here I am, thirty-six, and I'm still dreaming, still hoping and I've felt whatever talent I had withering. I have to try and send my roots rain, do you understand? I've spent my life wanting to be that impossible thing, an artist and I still want it more than anything. As for us and the German Terrorist and the blond young men who I seem to have a penchant for asking up here to be tied up—I have no answers, none at all! I want to stop working to define myself by every standard but mine. I want to stop judging myself. Some of us sit outside the standard categories our great society thinks so immutable. I have to find out what that particular truth is for me, or even if I have a truth. Maybe I create myself anew every time I sit down to mispell a new novel. I don't know. But I do know that we're finished. In the novel of my life your chapter is over and I have closed the book. So leave!

PATRICIA: No.

BEATRICE: All right, we'll toss for it.

PATRICIA: Oh, no—your randomness of art routine.

BEATRICE: Game?

PATRICIA: And my shrink says I have impulse problems.

BEATRICE: [*Challenging her*] You don't want to risk losing do you?

PATRICIA: Get the dice!

BEATRICE: [*Gets dice*] Call!

PATRICIA: [*Intent, despite herself*] Eight!

BEATRICE: Seven! [BEATRICE *woos the dice. He whispers to them, he caresses them, he kisses them, he holds them behind his back and hops, he lifts them to heaven and kneels repeating "seven, give me seven" over and over, he dances around* PATRICIA *like an Indian whooping "seven, give me seven"— in short he does everything he can to drive her crazy. He succeeds—she can bear it no longer.*]

PATRICIA: Stop! You're right! I don't want to risk losing!

BEATRICE: Told you, out!

PATRICIA: [*Preparing to leave*] It is sad never to have been loved but even sadder to be incapable of love.

BEATRICE: Isn't that a quote from Unamuno? You keep up that reading, Tricia, in between rubouts!

PATRICIA: And if you're having trouble writing have you ever thought it might be because you've lost your vulnerability? [PATRICIA, *feeling she has scored, sweeps out.* BEATRICE *cries after her:*]

BEATRICE: Vulnerability? Yo, fuck you, vulnerability! [*Silence. He slams the door and bolts it. He is alone in his new loft. He has dreamed of being here in just this spot. Now he doesn't know what to do. He takes the tape deck and rummages through the box of tapes. He selects a tape and plays it very loudly. It is* Das Lief von der Erde *by Mahler. Grand and sad music fills the room.* BEATRICE *pulls the armchair around and plugs in a light near it. He settles down, typewriter in lap to try and write. The storm which has been threatening bursts beyond the windows, there is thunder and lightning.* BEATRICE *is not having an easy time of it. Suddenly there is a banging at the door, accompanied by a loud hacking cough.*]

BEATRICE: [*Yelling over his music*] There's nobody home!

DY: [*Outside, coughing*] Please!

[BEATRICE *turns the tape off and listens. The coughing gets louder, there is a pathetic wheezing punctuating the nasty outbursts. Silence. Beatrice shrugs and is about to put the tape on again when more coughing explodes.* BEATRICE *opens the door.* ODYSSEUS MACDOWELL *is standing there, bedraggled, soaking wet, hungry, exhausted, slightly scared, and pretty sick.*]

BEATRICE: May I help you?

DY: Can I come in for a second? [*Coughs*] I'm sorry. These cops were chasing me, and the lobby door was ajar and I like ran up the stairs and yours is the top loft and I just need to sit down for a moment. [*Coughs. Takes his hat off.*] Please?

BEATRICE: You're just a kid!

DY: I'm a man! Fifteen years old—that's old enough to suffer, to kill, to die—I read *Soldier of Fortune*. [*He coughs and wheezes.*]

BEATRICE: Well ... look, I don't have a phone. There must be some kind of youth hostelry...

DY: I just escaped from one! That's why the cops were chasing me! They saw me sort of coughing in this doorway—I mean I have like minor allergies ... [*Coughs horribly, and shivers.*]

BEATRICE: Why did you escape?

DY: They were going to send me home and I won't go home!

BEATRICE: Are you in some kind of trouble?

DY: No. I had to be free.

BEATRICE: What?

DY: I had to be free! [*There is more thunder; rain beats against the windows.* DY *has edged his way in and is now inside the loft. Beatrice stands at the open door, not sure what to do.*]

BEATRICE: Look at all this rain. It's like Edgar Cayce.

DY: Edgar Cayce?

BEATRICE: [*Ironic*] He foresaw it all—earthquakes everywhere, planetary upheaval and near extinction for our sad race of humans. What I want to know is where we artists fit into all that. You're shivering.

DY: Do you like mind if I get warm, rest for a minute? I've got cough syrup from the hostelry and some pills. I also have a fifty in my hat so I can pay you something...

BEATRICE: [*Touched in spite of himself*] Well, my soon to be ex-wife brought some soup and tea. I never eat that stuff, so I can heat you some.

DY: Thank you. What do you eat?

BEATRICE: Haagen-Dazs, Sarah Lee and lots of coffee ... [DY *laughs*] What's so funny?

DY: You're so like Bohemian! [*Laughs then coughs*]

BEATRICE: My sometimes erratic but oftimes prescient common sense tells me this is some scam and as soon as I leave the room thirty of your tiny friends will break in and take everything but ... what the fuck, right? [*Goes off into the adjoining room where his kitchen is located to heat the soup and tea. DY takes off his Goodwill much too large overcoat now soaked—and his sneakers. He huddles up against the radiator and looks around. Now that an adult isn't present we can see that indeed he is frightened and sick, also determined not to be sent home or back to the hostelry. ODYSSEUS MACDOWELL, called DY by his friends, is a handsome boy, clearly from an upper class family. He takes himself very seriously. After a moment he takes a dog-eared notebook from deep within the overcoat, finds his pen and starts to write. BEATRICE enters with a blanket and towel.*] It'll be ready in a second. [*He hands DY the towel, DY dries himself, then wraps himself in the blanket and sits in the armchair, curling up, notebook in hand.*] Do you have a place to go or some friends in New York?

DY: No.

BEATRICE: Well, I was a conscientious objector medical orderly during the Viet Nam whatever, which doesn't make me a doctor but it looks to me like you have a middling case of bonchitis, and a heavy case of the runaways. Oops—I bet it's burning ... [*Rushes off into the kitchen. DY smiles to himself and makes notes in his book. There is more thunder and rain. DY looks back at the windows and realizes he doesn't have a place to go on what poromises to be a miserable night.* BEATRICE *enters with a cheap tray on which are soup and tea. There's also a glass of something which looks like milk.*]

BEATRICE: It wasn't burned—but it was a near thing. [*Putting the tray on* DY*'s lap.*] This is soup, this is tea. I thought you should have some milk but I don't have any so I put some half and half—I use it for coffee—in a glass and added some water. You don't have to drink it, it looks disgusting!

DY: Thanks. [*He smiles in what he hopes is a winning way at* BEATRICE.]

BEATRICE: [*Slightly unnerved*] Well, eat up!

DY: I'm waiting for it to like cool off.

BEATRICE: You might be better off burning your tongue, that way you won't taste it.

DY: Oh, like okay. [*Lifts spoon, blows on it, eats very slowly.*]

BEATRICE: You'll have to be on your way soon. I just moved in here and ... and I'm a writer. I work at night. *Alone.* I haven't done my page quota for today...

DY: [*Eating but interested*] You're like a writer?

BEATRICE: I'm trying to find out. My only other alternative is to go on a crash diet and become an airline steward.

DY: Might I have—well, you know—like heard of you?

BEATRICE: Depends on the circles you move in!

DY: I mean it! Are you like famous?

BEATRICE: Do I look like famous?

DY: What are your books?

BEATRICE: My big success, the one that sold well and even got made into a movie was *Little Boy Bound.* It started out as sort of a campy, kinky, children's book just as a joke but somehow it became a cult classic among adults.

DY: [*Slightly worried, looks around for chains.*] Little Boy Bound?

BEATRICE: It wasn't autobiographical.

DY: No?

BEATRICE: Not altogether. But like most sudden successes it diappeared quick...

DY: But what's your name?

BEATRICE: Bartholemew Dante.

DY: [*Impressed*] No!

BEATRICE: No?

DY: Like we read two of your stories in our "Antiquated Forms" seminar at St. Paul's.

BEATRICE: [*Savoring this*] Antiquated Forms?

DY: You know, like linear narrative, the pastorale, the eclogue, the conventional short story. My teacher thought your two stories were good examples of like last ditch efforts to save the form! God, a real writer! [*Writes enthusiastically in his notebook*]

BEATRICE: I feel a little sick to my stomach.

DY: Oh don't mind me. So, you're Bartholemew Dante!

BEATRICE: And what's your name?

DY: I hate telling real people my name.

BEATRICE: So what is it?

DY: Odysseus MacDowell. My brother's is worse—it's Trajan!

BEATRICE: Odysseus and Trajan! What did they call you around the house?

DY: Traje and Dy! Do you have any like siblings?

BEATRICE: A sister. Tracy. I called her Dick until she was seventeen then she broke my nose.

DY: [*After a moment*] Now, wait, that's an example of New York Ethnic Humor! [*Writes busily*]

BEATRICE: What is all this writing?

DY: Oh, please—don't like o.d. on my scribbling. You see, we had this old anthropologist at St. Paul's. He told us about the old days, and field work, and artifacts of culture and made us read Margaret Mead's *Coming of Age in Samoa.* It was real cool to find out what people did before, you know, television. So, I feel a little like an anthropologist taking notes in the field. [*Coughs*]

BEATRICE: Look ... what's your name?

DY: Dy.

BEATRICE: I hated my home too and ran away a lot but I never made the mistake of getting trapped too far away. That cough sounds terrible and this is not a great city to be alone and broke in—which I know from having been that a lot, only older than you. So you should take that fifty you said you had and go home...

DY: [*Seriously*] Oh, no, I'm never going back.

BEATRICE: But an underage runaway...?

DY: But I'm not a runaway. I've been in touch with my parents. I called them. I said: "Hello mom, hello dad, I'm okay," then I hung up.

BEATRICE: You hung up?

DY: I said goodbye first. My quarters had run out.

BEATRICE: They don't have collect calls?

DY: That's just it, they've been paying for me my whole life and I'm tired of it. I believe that kids should be put to work, sent out on their own at fifteen, younger even. School and all that crap is wasted on people like me. [*He realizes this may sound offensive to a writer.*] Look, it's not that I'm anti-intellectual or a video game nut—I'm distressed at all the semi-illiteracy around. But look, there's always the Public Library for books and there's well, you know, *life for the living*! Oh, like I know how goofy that sounds but I really mean it, sort of! I want to be in the real world, fighting and suffering, you understand? And joy, too, I'm not forgetting joy, but real life joys...

BEATRICE: There are no joys in real life.

DY: There have to be! So like, when I was fifteen—that was last August—the first segment of my trust fund came due. It was two thousand dollars! I invested it and all during Fall term I like plotted to escape St. Paul's, knowing in my bones that I had interest accruing! Then, in February, I fled! I mean I had had it ... And I'm a mature semi-sixteen year old, I don't need prepping and all that bullshit. I decided I'd hole up in New York. I hoarded all these back issues of like the *Village Voice* and I even found these old issues of like the *Soho Weekly News,* you know? They were in this dirty book store near St. Paul's—they charged me forty-six thirty-five for five of them—gave me like a discount on the sixth volume, you know? So I found out all I needed to know to like emigrate to New York City. And I'ts not like I'd never been here before. We'd come for plays, the museums and Brooks Brothers so I like knew the city. I got here and had like a great time for a while. I found this really cool room and I put my suitcases in there, and my walkman and my best cassettes, and my collectors issue of *Soldier of Fortune,* and then, like got back there one day and everything was gone. Like *everything*! Even the cash I'd hidden in my Prince cassette—you know *Purple Rain*—really rad! And when I ran down to the desk of the rooming house they said they had never seen me before and made me vacate that instant! I left, but at least I had this fifty I'd hidden in my hat! Then I wandered around in all this rain and got kind of sick, and these cops picked me up and took me to this hostelry. It was gross, like rancid to the max! It was full of old people, and crazy people—I was scared. And for a while they even refused to treat me because I wouldn't tell them my name or where I was from. It was like resisting torture. But then this social worker guy came on to me and asked me did I like to get high and maybe we could get together and I said sure, so he gave me the cough syrup and pills and then just as they were beginning to call around the country for missing person reports I skidaddled, like climbing over fences and breaking windows to get out of that place. It's horrible out, and I'm in a bad place, like I know that, but I'll die before I'll go home again and be rebuked by my parents, and burned by my brother, the great superstar Trajan. Like I hope I'm not boring you?

BEATRICE: No, I envy you. Just to be fifteen again and have all of life ahead of me.

DY: But you must have life ahead of you. What are you—twenty-eight?

BEATRICE: Thirty-six and defunct. Condemned to hell for not having learned from my mistakes. And speaking of mistakes, running away at fifteen is a bad one. I'm going to put some music on, you can rest for a second and then...

DY: Oh.

BEATRICE: Oh?

DY: Well, like I've been thinking. I mean, I have no place to go. I'm not really all that sick, mainly I was wet and tired, you know? And like all I need to completely recuperate is a day, maybe two at most, and this is—well—like a big loft ... [BEATRICE *laughs*] Even a night?

BEATRICE: Even a night! You don't know anything about me. I could be a killer, or a rapist of little boys.

DY: I'm not a little boy, I can take care of myself, and anyway your vibes are great!

BEATRICE: That's what the Piccadilly Prostitute said to Jack the ripper. Look, you can't stay here. I hate people but have a yen for boys—probably like that fellow who helped you at the hostelry...

DY: He was a creep but you...! Anyway, even despite the title of your novel, you don't seem like the kind of guy who'd force somebody...

BEATRICE: I'm not but it would be awkward at best...

DY: But...

BEATRICE: I mean it.

DY: [*After a moment's thought*] All right! Like, I'm sorry to have taken so much of your time. [*He starts getting dressed and gathering his things—very slowly.*] I like your toughness though.

BEATRICE: And what's so bad about your family? Do they abuse you?

DY: Oh, worse.

BEATRICE: Do drugs?

DY: Oh, much worse...

BEATRICE: [*Concerned*] What?

DY: They bore me. That's the worst. There should be a law against dull parents. Predictability, and like placidity, they're crimes, you know? My dad, for example. He's a killer at heart, but he only cries at funerals. I mean it. Soon as he sees a corpse in a coffin he starts to blubber. Especially if it's a stranger. My mother says: "If I had known your father was going to behave like that at funerals, I'd never have married him." Well—I'm like ready, sort of. [*He's fully dressed. He shakes* BEATRICE'*s hand in a decidedly funereal manner.*] Adios. And I guess now my father'll get to cry at a funeral— mine! [*Makes to leave but instead of going to the door, walks back to a window, opens it and climbs out onto the fire escape.*]

BEATRICE: Where are you going?

DY: [*Framed by the window, battered by rain and wind.*] I'm going to stand out in the rain until I die! [*Slams window shut and runs up the fire escape. We can hear* DY'*s anguished coughing from the fire escape.* BEATRICE *strides to the window, opens it, gets hit by rain and calls out to* DY.]

BEATRICE: You manipulative son of a bitch! Well, go ahead, stand out there. Someone's going to see you and call the police! [*Slams the window shut. He locks it. He goes to his typewriter, picks it up, rolls a page in. Thunder, lightning, coughing. Rain hits the window.* BEATRICE *feels guilty. Wads up the paper and goes to the window.*] Yo, kid! [DY *peeks down, as though not sure he is the one addressed.*] Yes you!

You see any other kids out there? Come back in!
[DY *climbs in, soaking wet, shivering and coughing.* BEA-
TRICE *slams the window shut.* DY *doffs his coat, seizes the
towel and the blanket.*]
BEATRICE: Goddamned Catholic Church! I was raised to feel
guilty and I hate it! But I'm not going to let you stay here!
[*Addressing Heaven*] Do you hear me, Virgin Mary? [*He
looks over at the feverish* DY *who is huddling under the
blanket. He fights an internal war, aware that the boy has no
place to go and is perhaps on the brink of being seriously ill.
On the other hand he hates being a sucker.* DY *looks at him,
clearly in need.*] I have it! The dice!
DY: [*Surprised*] The dice?
BEATRICE: I used to believe in the randomness of art when I was
in school.
DY: When was that?
BEATRICE: The Renaissance, when do you think? Randomness of
art was very *au courant* back then...
DY: [*Laying it on thick*] Randomness of art ... the dice ... what
a strange new world this is.
BEATRICE: Pardon me while I puke.
DY: [*Manipulatively*] You're real hard to manipulate!
BEATRICE: [*Firm*] Stop trying then! So I tell you what: We'll toss
for it, two out of three. If your number comes up you can
stay until you feel a little better, subject to an hour to hour
renewal. If my number comes up you have to leave and
where you go is your business and I refuse to feel guilty.
DY: Like, do you always do this? Is everything random?
BEATRICE: In life, probably, in art, probably not! Ready?
DY: [*Very serious*] Let me take some cough medicine. [*He takes a
swig, concentrates—this is life or death for him.*] I'm ready!
BEATRICE: [*Sarcastic*] Do you want to invoke the WASP God or
sing doxology or something?
DY: You're a slightly cruel tease, aren't you? My father and
brother are that way, they can make my mother cry, but like,
don't worry, I've built up defenses. But like, you know,
wouldn't it be a lot easier if you just sort of let me stay?
BEATRICE: Oh, no!
DY: Why?
BEATRICE: That would involve choice.

DY: What's wrong with choice?

BEATRICE: Trust me, chance is better. Call!

DY: [*Desperately trying to think of a lucky number.*] Seven!

BEATRICE: Nine! [BEATRICE *throws, they look at the dice intently.*] Three doesn't mean anything. Call!

DY: [*After a moment's thought*] Seven!

BEATRICE: [*Thinks*] Three! [BEATRICE *throws; the dice land a little away from them, they scramble after them, and read them intently.*] Three, I won!

DY: It's two out of three, remember!

BEATRICE: Your odds are shrinking. Call!

DY: [*Thinks*] Seven!

BEATRICE: You have a lot of faith in seven!

DY: Shut up and call!

BEATRICE: [*Thinks*] Four! [BEATRICE *woos the dice. He whispers to them between cupped hands, he strokes them, he kisses them.* DY *becomes more and more anxious.*]

DY: What are you doing?

BEATRICE: Wooing fate, you mind? What was your call?

DY: Seven!

BEATRICE: Four! [BEATRICE *throws the dice but* DY *throws himself on top of them and scatters them.*] What are you doing?

DY: [*Recovering the dice*] You've thrown every time, it was my turn! Call!

BEATRICE: [*Thinks, then deliberately chooses* DY's *number.*] Seven!

DY: Four! [DY *woos the dice in imitation of* BEATRICE, *maybe going a little further since staying has come to mean a lot to him.* BEATRICE *becomes impatient.*]

BEATRICE: Will you throw for Christ's sake!? [DY *starts to throw, then suddenly moves across the room.*] Where are you going?

DY: I felt unlucky there! Call!

BEATRICE: Seven!

DY: Four! [DY *throws, they both rush after the dice to read them.*] Four! Four! I won!

BEATRICE: [*A little rattled*] It's two out of three, remember!

DY: [*Triumphant*] *Your* odds are shrinking!

BEATRICE: [*Irritated*] Give me the dice! [BEATRICE *snatches the*

dice away from DY.] Call!
DY: [*Suddenly very nervous*] Uh ... uh...
BEATRICE: [*Fierce*] Will you call, damn you!?
DY: Six!
BEATRICE: [*Thinks*] Five! [BEATRICE *woos the dice, rather seriously this time, then throws. They both run after the dice and read intently.*]
DY: Six?! You mean it, six?! I won—I won! [*He leaps up and down for joy with such intensity that he has a coughing fit. Then settling down a bit.*] I won.
BEATRICE: [*Primly*] It wasn't a contest so nobody won! [*Picks up the dice*] Goddamn superstition, I should have learned from the Church! [BEATRICE *throws the dice out the window.*]
DY: Look, don't go to any trouble for me. I'll just lie here—if you have some rags I'll lie on them.
BEATRICE: Rags? Yo, fuck you, rags! What have you been reading, Dickens? I have a rollaway bed for when my mother visits, I also have a rollaway life for when she visits, but that's another story. [*Gets rollaway bed from one of the rooms and pushes it on stage.*] I don't have any spare bedding, so this'll have to do. Just don't get too comfortable—remember words like temporary, evanescent, ephemeral—think in terms of hours, or better, minutes...
DY: I get you, absolutely ... [*Tries to repress a coughing spasm, and shivers.*] Can I like take a hot shower?
BEATRICE: I suppose. [DY *starts to undress*] Oh no—I'm going to have to buy stuff for breakfast! [BEATRICE *shudders involuntarily at the very notion.*] I'm broke—can I borrow some of your fifty?
DY: [*Handing him the money*] Sure, take what you need. Breakfast—God, that sounds good! But like, can I have a snack now?
BEATRICE: Certainly. I have Sarah Lee chocolate pound cake, vanilla swiss-almond Haagen-Dazs, and diet Pepsi!
DY: I'll wait for breakfast. A real Italian breakfast!
BEATRICE: A real Italian breakfast?
DY: You're Italian, aren't you? Sausages and peppers and eggs ... [BEATRICE *shakes his head*] What do you have for breakfast?
BEATRICE: Sarah Lee and Haagen-Dazs unless I'm being nutritious then I have orange cake Sarah Lee and something with raisins in it.

DY: Well, at the deli get a few eggs for me, and orange juice—
without sugar and something with bran in it. [BEATRICE *looks
irritable*] I'll take my shower now ... [*Runs into the
bathroom*]
[BEATRICE *heaves a sigh, unhappy about having a guest, then
puts on his overcoat. There is more thunder and lightning.
BEATRICE takes an umbrella and goes to the loft door. There
is a knock at the door.*] What is it?
PUER'S VOICE: [*Outside*] Please!
[BEATRICE *opens the door. He sees a boy—fourteen at most—
standing there, drenched. The boy is blond but seems to have
some Italian mixed in. He is wearing a knapsack; his clothes
have a somewhat foreign, institutional look to them, but are
good quality. PUER is a formidably poised child, with a
German accent. His English is clear, very accurate and quite
formal—not quite idiomatic.*]
BEATRICE: [*Puzzled and somehow knowing this is not a good
sign.*] Who are you?
PUER: Who are you?
BEATRICE: You first.
PUER: Are you Bartholemew Dante?
BEATRICE: Naturally.
PUER: And fourteen years ago you were with Henrietta Schluss-
nuss?
BEATRICE: Who?
PUER: Henrietta Schlussnuss, a German woman with Leftist
leanings and a gift for organization. And you fathered a
child with her? A male child?
BEATRICE: This is a practical joke ... [*Looks out into the
hallway*] Come out of hiding Patricia, I don't think this is
funny! Where is she?
PUER: Who?
BEATRICE: The sick lady who hired you...
PUER: Are these idioms? I am sorry so to trouble you, but I have
tried every way to contact you. I wrote you at your former
publisher, they returned the letters with "Address Unknown"
on them. I tried your former residence but they said you had
disappeared. I escaped from Germany last week and arrived
here by unconventional means, determined to find you. I
went to all the colleges and universities certain you were

teaching. Everywhere was I turned away, you were unknown. But, last week, whilst roaming the corridors at City
College, I chanced to ask a blond boy named Arnold if he
had ever heard of you. He had. He said he was coming to see
you today to discover the true meaning of your fine book
Little Boy Bound and he gave me this address, only
cautioning me to wait several hours after his appointment. I
have done so, but am now exhausted, and wet and out of
money. I don't want to go back to Germany without seeing
you. Father, I am your son. [BEATRICE, *stunned, stands in the
doorway.* PUER *not sure of his welcome but unwilling to
stand in the hallway edges in, and doffs his knapsack. He
looks around the loft, then back at* BEATRICE. *He opens his
arms.* BEATRICE *slams the door and faces* PUER.]

BEATRICE: Prove it! [*Without a word,* PUER *retrieves a folder of
photographs from his knapsack. They show* BEATRICE *with*
HENRIETTA *and the baby* PUER, *many years ago.* BEATRICE
scrutinizes these.] I don't believe you. You could have ripped
these pictures off some poor half-Italian kid. [*He drags* PUER
to the lamp and stares at him under the light.] You look like
Henrietta, she was just as terrifying but no—

PUER: Indeed, I am your seed in flesh. Puer Schlussnuss Dante.

BEATRICE: Oh yes? Okay, how did we come up with the name
Puer?

PUER: Well, as my mother, Henrietta the Terrorist narrates it,
you were flirting with a Wagnerian name. You were going to
name me Wehwalt, that is Woeful, from *Die Walkure* but
then, when I was four months old and quite without a name
as yet, you were watching a Tarzan movie on television. I
believe it was the one where Tarzan finds a son. They name
him Boy. Puer is Latin for boy.

BEATRICE: [*Horrified*] I had forgotten that horrible story! Where's
your mother now?

PUER: In prison, of course.

BEATRICE: What did she do this time?

PUER: She abducted the entire cast, crew, and conductor and
director of a new *Gotterdammerung* in Frankfurt. She did
not think they stressed Wagner's fascistic leanings enough
and also felt the conductor and soprano were annihilating
the score. She is a terrorist with artistic pretensions.

BEATRICE: Like a critic! Well ... Puer ... I guess you are the consequence of my whatever with Henrietta ... [*Involuntarily beats his breast and groans.*] Would you like some Haagen-Dazs and Sarah Lee?

PUER: These are code words for drugs?

BEATRICE: In a manner of speaking.

PUER: I will eat my bran bar, thank you! [*Takes a bar from his knapsack.*]

BEATRICE: [*Not pleased*] Oh dear God, he's eating bran!

PUER: [*Gesturing toward the rollaway*] May I use this bed, father?

BEATRICE: Look ... Puer—what kind of person would name his son Puer? Look, I just moved in here and I'm having trouble working. You know I write ... wrote...

PUER: I read all your published works. Only *Little Boy Bound* was translated, but I found the others and read them in English.

BEATRICE: [*In spite of himself*] What did you think?

PUER: I thought them the product of a noble struggle to marry a perfervid, erratic imagination with an acute if unsteady sense of reality. Some bran?

BEATRICE: Well ... son ... Puer ... kid ... young man ... I really, that is ... really don't think ... sort of...

PUER: You do not wish me to stay here.

BEATRICE: Yes.

PUER: I understand totally.

BEATRICE: You do?

PUER: Oh yes. You see, on the computer I analyzed your likely response from what I could discover about you. By reading interviews for example. I factored in your writings, I took into account your age, and the widely publicized aberrations of your generation in America—the futile pseudo-political movements of the sixties, abuse of drugs and so on. You are behaving exactly as I saw indicated on the screen.

BEATRICE: I am getting a headache. Where did you go to school?

PUER: I was raised in homes in Germany. After a time I was tested and discovered to possess certain native abilities. A group of us, gifted discards so to speak, were segregated and given intensive coaching in computer technology. Then we studied to become computers. We were taught that love and other human feelings were only experienced by rodent-brained primitives whom we had surpassed. The individual, the family, the tribe have all passed away, so what use have we of the crocodile brain?

BEATRICE: Excuse me, I have to scream. [*Screams*] That's better.

PUER: But you see, *I* feel, *I* hope. I could not bear those homes. I want to experience this earth before it is changed or destroyed by war. They taught us English and Chinese, feeling those to be the linguistic constructs of the future and since I have an American passport, I came here. For who does not wish to see his father once? Having seen my father, and touched him [*Touches* BEATRICE] I can start to know that I truly am human, and belong on the earth.

BEATRICE: Well—[*Doesn't know what to think about all this but is sure he doesn't want* PUER *staying with him.*] I'm going to call my ex-wife Patricia. She has a huge lovely duplex on Madison Avenue—you'd like it there. She has cats, dogs, snakes and several brothers—you can entertain yourself trying to tell them apart. That's all right?

PUER: [*Disappointed, but hiding it*] Certainly.

BEATRICE: You can take this video game I invented.

PUER: As in *Pac-Man?*

BEATRICE: *Death in Venice.* [*Wheels in the video game he has designed. He plugs it in, hands one control to* PUER, *takes the other himself, turns the game on and explains it.*] You see, there's the little boy ... [*High pitched noises*] There's the old man ... [*Middle register noises*] and there's the cholera ... [*Deep, blob-like noises. They play for a minute. Cholera wins. A victory song is heard from the machine then a deep voice intoning: "Got you, faggot."*] You can play with this ... I don't have a phone so I'll have to go to the corner and call her. You're sure you don't mind?

PUER: It is enough to have seen you, my father. And if in the coming days we may talk again that will enhance my pleasure. [BEATRICE *full of guilt and touched in spite of himself, runs out.* PUER *removes his coat and starts investigating the game.* DY *enters, having finished his shower. He is carrying his clothes and is wrapped in a towel.*]

DY: Who are you?

PUER: Puer Schlussnuss Dante. Who are you?

DY: Odysseus MacDowell. [*An awkward pause. Neither knows*

what to make of the other. DY *goes to the bed,* PUER *plays with the game, furtively glancing over at* DY. DY *is determined to be cool and ignore this stranger.* PUER *decides to break the ice.*]

PUER: So, you are having sexual congress with my father?

DY: [*Stunned*] What?

PUER: [*Very friendly*] I intuit from the context that you and he are intimate. [*Registering the shock on* DY*'s face but misinterpreting it.*] It is no surprise. Firstly, my mother, Henrietta the Terrorist, told me of my father's probable inversion and potentially embarrassing tastes, calculating when I confided in her my hopes for escape from Germany, that he might like me better now than if I waited. Secondly, it is a leitmotif in his writings.

DY: What are you talking about?

PUER: I am the son of your erastes!

DY: My who?

PUER: The older man who is teaching you the ways of manhood in the manner of Classical Greece.

DY: I have a headache.

PUER: This was once quite a common arrangement and did not necessarily denote exclusive homosexuality but now it is regarded as eccentric, no? [*Realizing that* DY *looks speechless with horror*] Am I lacking in tact, perhaps?

DY: I just came in for a shower and a snack. And you mean he has a son?

PUER: Sexuality does not move in discrete patterns. But tell me, you mean you are not his boy concubine?

DY: No way!

PUER: A pity!

DY: Why?

PUER: Then we would be brothers in a sense. It would be nice to have a brother, even one begat under eccentric circumstances.

DY: I already have a brother.

PUER: [*Very interested*] And how is that?

DY: Overrated.

PUER: You do not love him?

DY: Oh, chill out! Love him?

PUER: Brothers should love one another.

DY: He pushed me out of a second story window when we were kids—that's how much he loved me.

PUER: A monster! Was he severely punished?

DY: Are you kidding? This is America! No one gets punished. They didn't even invent a WASP punishment like no dessert or no TV. And you know who got sent to the child shrink?

PUER: [*Not knowing the word*] Shrink?

DY: Like psychologist.

PUER: Who?

DY: I did, that's who! Mom and Dad decided Trajan was such an angel that I must have done something like monstrous to the max to incite him to throw me out the window.

PUER: Did it help?

DY: What?

PUER: The shrinking?

DY: Of course not, I'm mental health on parade!

PUER: [*Thinks for a minute*] Beg pardon, but have you Latin ancestors?

DY: No, why?

PUER: From where comes the name Trajan?

DY: It's an old family name like Odysseus. I'm called Dy by the way. [*They shake hands*] What's your name—Puer? Where did they come up with that?

PUER: It is Latin for boy.

DY: Oh, like you're a generic kid.

PUER: Is that an idiom?

DY: I wonder if I should get dressed and like book. There won't be room for me now...

PUER: No. I doubt I'll be staying here. But tell me—do you imply it is not good to have a brother? For you see I have dreamed awake about having a brother. I wished for a love so to speak, not erotic in nature, such as might arise from those of the same seed. I wished to feel less singular and alone.

DY: I've never felt singular and alone, and if I did my brother sure wouldn't help! You are one weird dude.

PUER: That is good yes? And now I must use the facilities.

DY: [*Pointing through the door*] They're in there. [PUER *goes through the door.* DY *is left looking after him shaking his head. He is about to remove his towel and get dressed when the front door opens.* PATRICIA, DANNY *and* BEATRICE *enter having come for* PUER. PATRICIA *determinately making the best of it approaches* DY, *hand outstretched, thinking he is* PUER.]

PATRICIA: [*To* DY] How are you Puer? I'm Patricia Giambattista Dante, and you're going to be staying with me awhile. [DY, *amazed, takes her hand. She, moved by her own good will grabs him into an embrace which effectively loosens his towel, he pulls it around himself while* PATRICIA *turns to* DANNY.] Danny, get his stuff.

DY: But ... [*Looks to the horrorstruck* BEATRICE *for help, in vain.*]

DANNY: This kid looks old enough to take care of himself. [PUER *returns from the bathroom.*]

PUER: Father, you have returned.

PATRICIA: [*Shocked, to* PUER] You're his son? [PUER *nods yes.* PATRICIA *then points to* DY.] Who's that? [*There is an abashed silence.* PATRICIA *takes in* DY, *his age, his towel, then turns to* BEATRICE *who is clearly praying to disappear.*] You filthy pervert!

BLACKOUT. END OF ACT ONE

ACT TWO

[BEATRICE'*s loft, a week after Act One. It is early afternoon.
The loft looks more settled.* DY'*s rollaway, unmade, is against a
wall.* BEATRICE *sits on a box, his typewriter in his lap. He is
trying to work—not too successfully from the look of it.
Crumpled papers lie on the floor around him. Mahler is once
again playing on the tape deck.* BEATRICE *looks over at the
unmade bed. Suddenly* DY *bursts into the loft. He is fully
recovered. He is wearing his coat and hat. He is very excited.*]

DY: Beatrice, I got a job! I got a job!

BEATRICE: Great! Can I have a loan? Just joking. What is it?

DY: Well—when did we meet? Was that last Monday? Well,
starting Wednesday I started making the rounds looking for
jobs. It was awful. Everywhere it was the same: "You're too
young, you don't have enough experience." Like my fake I.D.
did no good at all—and I paid twenty-four thirty for it on
Times Square! And they wouldn't believe me when I lied
about experience. I mean, like I told people I'd been in the
Marine Corps and they'd just snicker. There's no patriotism
left in our country, you know? So, by Saturday morning I was
near despair and I decided I needed a high-fat with sugar junk
feast. Like my chemistry teacher last fall said that was the best
way to get high without using drugs. So I went into this
Mickey D's...

BEATRICE: Mickey D's?

DY: Like McDonald's—the new one with huge glass windows on
Spring Street. So, I'm finishing my Chicken McNuggets then I
see this sign—it was like a sign from heaven in an old movie!
For Hire—it says. So I filled out the forms and went in to see
the manager. His eyes like popped out when he saw me. He
said: "You are the first Anglo ever to fill out the forms!" I
didn't know what an Anglo was then I flashed on it. Like I was
the first white boy ever to fill out the forms! I'll tell you I felt
like some explorer entering alien terrain. So the manager said:
"Come back on Monday morning." So I went back this
morning—you were still asleep, and the head of hiring was
there. And he said I looked just like the boy in the commercial
and I would be great for business because the Soho McDon-

ald's is meant to be an upscale place. And they put me right into management training, and while I'm learning to run the place I get to stand right in the middle of the store and smile! Like this, see? [*Smiles*] So I got a job, I'm employed, I'm like an adult! It's really got me like *irked*! [*Pulls* BEATRICE *into a joyful dance*]

BEATRICE: [*Not understanding the idiom*] Irked?

DY: Like, overjoyed! And the thing is if I get a paycheck or two under my belt I'll be able to afford a nice room, maybe even a tenement apartment! Just flash on that, me in a tenement, isn't that fierce!

BEATRICE: Fierce indeed. [*He ruffles* DY'*s hair.* DY *smiles back at him.*]

DY: I can bring guests sort of like under the table, you know— they all do it so you could like eat with me for free.

BEATRICE: At McDonalds? Thanks.

DY: [*Gets his notebook*] I've got to write all this down! [*Starts to write.* BEATRICE *goes back to his typewriter, reads what he has written and rips it out of the roller and tears it up.* DY *looks up at him.*]

DY: I guess it's not great for you to have me around. So, I'll be out of your hair soon.

BEATRICE: I suppose that's for the best, all told.

DY: I've had fun being here though. Even if that opera last night was pretty rad.

BEATRICE: Rad?

DY: You know, radical?

BEATRICE: *Hansel and Gretel* radical? [*Thinks about that and shrugs*]

DY: And your friends in standing room were pretty weird.

BEATRICE: We always cry when the little boys come out of the Gingerbread.

DY: There were some little girls in there, too.

BEATRICE: We don't cry over them. but how can you say you had fun? You hated it.

DY: Oh—but like just hanging out with all of you was so crazy. I mean sneaking in with those fairies—I mean strange gentle-men with knapsacks—then stealing those seats, and being chased out of them—all those freaks—well, like opera lovers in the standing room and then sitting around in that dirty restaurant afterwards where those two fa... men started screaming at each other over this dead singer I had never heard of—that was wild! And like nobody batted an eye because I'm a teenager or treated me like a child. That one man even insisted I agreed with him about the singer I had never heard of. I wrote it all down in my notebook last night—and believe me it all added up to fun!

BEATRICE: I've had fun with you, too. Chaste fun. I've gotten into the habit of thinking that a contradiction in terms. And I'm amazed I've enjoyed having you around so much.

DY: Why?

BEATRICE: Everybody always said I couldn't tolerate intimacy. In the old days I'd fine Patricia if she didn't keep to her end of the duplex from dawn to dusk. Of course she was so busy with her career she didn't mind.

DY: Boy that's so different from anything I ever heard of in Greenwich, Connecticut. Didn't she hate you?

BEATRICE: Oh no—she's still trying to hang on to me—though I guess it's for political reasons now. She's running for Congress in a few months and doesn't want it to get around that she had a fag for a husband.

DY: But, like it doesn't compute in my head. You were married yet you kind of kept her away from you...

BEATRICE: No, we were great friends. See, that's one of the problems of life. Sorting out friendship and love and sex. We grew up together in South Philadelphia. She developed sort of a crush on me. I don't know why, I was homely as sin in those days. I used to think, how ironic, the prettiest girl in her class at Saint Maria Goretti's High School adores me and not one football player will look at me twice, even the trolls.

DY: God—go a little slower. I'm writing this down!

BEATRICE: She and I would talk for hours. It was comfortable for both of us because sex was never an issue. You have to realize we were raised Catholic before Vatican Two and that meant lots of lust-loathing. Oh those nuns! Those nuns! [DY *laughs in delight and anticipation.*]

DY: Tell me about them. I've never known anybody who had nuns for teachers. [*Writes what* BEATRICE *tells him.*]

BEATRICE: Well, I still remember my first erection in public ... aren't you going to be late for work?

DY: They just want me to come in for a little while later this afternoon. Members of the Community Board are going to be there. Go on!

BEATRICE: Well, my first erection in public was during afternoon prayers in Sister Mary Emyard's eighth grade class—do you think I matured late? We were all standing beside our little desks and saying the "Our Father" for the conversion of China, and I popped this boner...

DY: Boner? That's fifties slang for...

BEATRICE: You got it! Well, sister saw it. I'm not bragging—I was at the first desk and she had an eagle eye. She swoops down on me, grabs me by the ear, pulls me up to the front of the class, calls me a filthy pig, kneels in front of me so that she is eye level with my crotch, prays to the Holy Virgin to take it away, then forces me under her desk, sits down and squeezes my head between her knees.

DY: God, that must be why you're gay!

BEATRICE: No, that's why I can't spell or add and know tons of dirty details about hundreds of saints who never even existed.

DY: Like I'm trying to imagine growing up like that. When we were in Junior High School we had some women teachers— some of them were fierce, but some were sexy in that schoolteacher-like prim kind of way, you know? I'd like daydream about them taking me to their houses for detention and ... well you know, once we were there alone. The thing is that though they were like teachers and all—they were women too, real women with some kind of sex about them. But those nuns—it sounds like they were anti-women. Having them must have made making it with a woman real tough—I'm surprised you were able to at all.

BEATRICE: Oh, there are great things about heterosexuality.

DY: [*Poised to write*] What for instance?

BEATRICE: Don't you know? I thought you were straight?

DY: I'm straight, I'm straight, but I'd like an older man's opinion.

BEATRICE: What makes heterosexuality great—let me think, let me think ... Well, a woman's body.

DY: What's it like?

BEATRICE: Well, mysterious for starters. Talk about being an explorer entering alien terrain. The body changes so completely depending on how you kiss her or touch her. No sex education class or porno book prepares you for that. And lying with her at night, hearing her breathe, feeling safe and protective at the same time, having all that warmth around you ... that's amazing.

DY: Can you have that with a guy?

BEATRICE: You're asking the wrong person ... of course you can, of course you can. Those two guys last night who were screaming at each other over that singer you never heard of have been together for twenty years and they have that kind of intimacy; so do other men I know. But I've never found it for myself, I told you, intimacy seems impossible for me. For some strange reason I found it briefly and not too happily with two genital females. But I always felt a little false; if I wasn't acting a hundred percent I was acting forty or fifty percent. There was always this suffocating longing inside me for something else—not someone else but something else entirely— I'd see a man, or more likely a boy on the street, or have fleeting sex with one and endure months of longing ... But those things never worked out, I used to think it was because I was ugly, or a bore, or lousy sex—and there probably is some truth in all that. But, it may be because I am a half-person, who hovers over real life but never lands firmly and unequivocably in any known category of behavior. And now, I doubt I'll ever have any intimacy with a male. With this damned disease AIDS, death comes in the guise of the beautiful youth and your love gift can be a wasting disease. And somehow I've got to find a center, a reason for living on...

DY: [*Not having understood entirely, yet touched, wanting to comfort* BEATRICE.] You're unhappy.

BEATRICE: Oh fuck unhappy! What human's got a right to be happy? I'm talking emptiness ... now get out of here, start your climb up the corporate ladder. Let me try to work and fail some more!

DY: [*Would rather stay but realizes* BEATRICE *means it. He gathers his things, a little sad on* BEATRICE's *account.*] I'll be back early; maybe I'll bring a surprise—Yo! [DY *runs out.* BEATRICE *looks after* DY *with longing, he shakes his head, gets up and puts the tape deck on. With trepidation he returns to the typewriter and rolls another piece of paper in. The front door swings open.* PATRICIA *strides in with* DANNY *behind her.* DANNY *is carrying a phone.*]

PATRICIA: [*To* BEATRICE] I brought you a phone. Yo, Danny, find the jack and plug it in.

BEATRICE: I don't want a phone. Besides, don't you need the phone company?

DANNY: [*Seeking the jack*] I took a course, just be patient.

PATRICIA: We passed your little inamorato on the stairs...

DANNY: That kid's a killer, I can tell.

BEATRICE: There is nothing between us!

PATRICIA: Oh sing me another aria, have you tied him up yet? Does he know what a sicko you are?

DANNY: [*To* PATRICIA, *having found the jack*.] Yo, boss, show some respect! There's nothin' wrong with a little tying up. Look at all the times I been tied up, never did me no harm. [*He's connected the phone*] And Beatrice is good people. He can tie me up anytime he wants.

PATRICIA: Oh, does your girlfriend know that, Danny?

DANNY: That's what I can't understand about this society! Straight, gay, who gives a fuck, hanh? No disrespect, but what's the big deal?

BEATRICE: [*To* PATRICIA] You see, even your goon has more humanity than you!

PATRICIA: Yo, Danny—you hooked up yet?

DANNY: Yep.

PATRICIA: Go downstairs, turn on the juice, then wait outside for Pasquale—he should be here in ten minutes!

DANNY: Pasquale! Poor Beatrice. Yo! [*Exits*]

PATRICIA: [*To* BEATRICE] I brought you this phone because I thought you might like to call your son. He came with us.

BEATRICE: Where is he?

PATRICIA: At the supermarket. He calls it the museum of our time. He decided he shouldn't come calling without gifts, so he's buying Sarah Lee and Haagen-Dazs and diet Pepsi ... with my money. Are you going to let him move in?

BEATRICE: Oh, God, don't start, Patricia!

PATRICIA: You're a disgrace! It's been a week, a whole fuckin' week. You've been holed up here with your baby whore doing the Kama Sutra according to Bartholemew Dante and meanwhile your own son is sitting in some stranger's apartment waiting for you. I'm trying to start my campaign, I can't look after him and I resent having to look after him.

BEATRICE: I'm sorry. He should go back to Germany.

PATRICIA: Back to Germany?

BEATRICE: Well, he was raised there, they support him...

PATRICIA: Didn't he tell you what that school was like? It sounds grisly. Maybe this is big mama Tricia talking, but how can you abandon your own son like that?

BEATRICE: I already abandoned him—fourteen years ago.

PATRICIA: I thought it was Henrietta who stole him?

BEATRICE: She took him with her, but I certainly didn't try to track them down, or get him back. I was relieved. [PATRICIA *can't disguise her disapproval*] My son—isn't that all bullshit? There's no psychic emanation from him that would draw me to him on a crowded subway. And I certainly have to believe he's better off in that school however chilling it may sound to children of the sixties like us, than he ever would be with me.

PATRICIA: But when you chase after boys for sex—maybe it's him you're looking for?

BEATRICE: Fire your shrink, Patricia, his notion is that life is one big fat woman and all it needs is reduction. I do not chase boys for sex. The few teenagers I've had sexual congress with were as big as I am, no more than a few months under the age of consent in New York City, and in truth chased me.

PATRICIA: Fine. I didn't say you were a rapist. But you have to grant me the fantasy is there...

BEATRICE: The fantasy is mysterious in its origins like all sexual tastes. But if it is rooted in anything it is rooted in my sense of myself...

PATRICIA: What do you mean?

BEATRICE: When you look in the mirror what do you see?

PATRICIA: An adult. What do you see?

BEATRICE: A teenager—a child, someone with his whole life ahead of him. I broke away from you because I felt like you were mama. And that pattern spells failure. I need to grow up, I need to raise myself. And to have a needy little boy, a *peculiar* needy boy around would make that impossible.

PATRICIA: That's just like a man's bullshit! It's so selfish!

BEATRICE: Selfish? Yo, fuck you, selfish! What do you know about responsibility?

PATRICIA: I know plenty!

BEATRICE: Oh yes, a two-bit hoodlum's daughter. When did you ever want for anything? Or have to lift a finger? And now

daddums has made some money, and has a few people scared
and suddenly he's sending his baby to Congress! What do you
know about anything human? You didn't even want a real
marriage. So don't hand me any of your born-again Italian
mama bullshit! This is the man you lived with...

PATRICIA: The man I lived with was a profoundly decent man,
full of courage however confused he might have been. The
man I lived with transcended his sexuality. You've become a
stereotype—a stupid queen!

BEATRICE: Oh, fuck you, you frigid bitch! Why don't you go out
and find somebody with balls to marry then come back and
preach to me about normalcy?

PATRICIA: You used to have balls!

BEATRICE: And I don't understand this trip from you. You were
the one who never wanted a real husband, who never wanted a
child...

PATRICIA: You were my child! [*Bursts into tears*]

BEATRICE: Now, Patricia, don't cry...

PATRICIA: All these accusations are so unfair; you of all people—
you, my oldest friend, know my father didn't buy off the Law
School, or set up my practice and running for office, that's
something I've always wanted to do...

BEATRICE: Well if those tears are real you might think about
severing your ties to organized crime!

PATRICIA: [*Recovering herself*] Oh, fuck organized crime! It's no
different from the IRS. [*The door opens.* PUER *stands on the
threshold, carrying a shopping bag. From it he takes a carton
of Haagen-Dazs. He poses with it, then moves toward*
BEATRICE, *singing Siegmund's words from Act One of* Die
Walkure.]

PUER: "Kuelende Labung gab mir der Quell, des Mueden Lust
machte er leicht; erfrischt ist der Mut, das Aug'erfreut, des
Sehens selige Lust...* [*He ends up in front of* BEATRICE *and
sweetly but grandly hands him the Haagen-Dazs.*]

BEATRICE: You have to get over that Wagner!

---

*Puer is punning. In Act One he reminded Beatrice that the first name his parents
considered for him was Wehwalt—Woeful—one of Siegmund's aliases in *Die
Walkure*. These words are sung by the wounded Siegmund, a warrior-poet
searching for his long lost twin sister (as Puer has been searching for his father)
both of them having been abandoned by their father, as Puer was. Siegmund has
just been given water by Sieglinde—his twin—who he hasn't as yet recognized.

PUER: I am going to *Die Walkure* this evening, Patricia purchased a seat for me, but I have time for a visit, my father.

PATRICIA: I'll leave you two alone. Beatrice, my brother Pasquale wants to talk to you. I'll bring him up. [*Leaves*]

BEATRICE: Well, Puer, I hope you are good at first aid, they are probably going to break my legs.

PUER: Oh? They have seemed very genteel to me.

BEATRICE: But of course, nowadays they use sani-wipes before and after hits.

PUER: [*Retrieving shopping bag*] I have brought us luncheon. [*He removes Sarah Lee cake, diet Pepsi, and opens the carton of Haagen-Dazs.*] How is Odysseus?

BEATRICE: Employed.

PUER: Are you and he ... any closer?

BEATRICE: In a sense.

PUER: And in another sense?

BEATRICE: No, and we're not going to be.

PUER: How is your writing?

BEATRICE: Dreadful.

PUER: I saw in this rather charming local newspaper, the *Village Voice,* an advertisement for the film version of *Little Boy Bound.* It is playing at the Eighth Street Playhouse.

BEATRICE: Yes, as part of their festival of the Greatest Movie Bombs in history. I didn't even get to write the screenplay. They paid some Hollywood hack half a million to write it. But since everyone thinks it was a joke what difference does it make?

PUER: Yes, there was a slighting reference to your work in that same issue of the *Village Voice.* But I am fond of *Little Boy Bound* and my feeling is not simple filial loyalty. You see, I stole it in Germany.

BEATRICE: You stole it?

PUER: I could not buy it—no money. It was in Munich. Out of the home they let us go free one day a week. The other boys went to a small eating place in the mall where *Laverne and Shirley* and *Happy Days* were shown in English. But I went to the bookstores. I learned to steal very politely. I stole all your books, and we read them at the home, after lights out. It was tempting to dismiss you as a middle level fabulist with an eccentric streak. But to do that was to read you superficially.

For, despite the silliness of your plots I felt, beating under your work, a heart and a mind. It is clearest in your two books of poems, especially the second one influenced by Gerard Manley Hopkins, and Rilke.

BEATRICE: [*Impressed*] You got that?

PUER: Of course. But even in *Little Boy Bound* there was much charm and wit.

BEATRICE: There was also a lot of bondage but perhaps we shouldn't discuss that...

PUER: There was great symbolic appeal. At the end...

BEATRICE: What scene? The one where the extraterrestrial bad guys, Mallarme and Debussey have tied up two boy scout troops, a bunch of cub scouts, and all the raw recruits at a Marine boot camp?

PUER: Precisely!

BEATRICE: Boy, did I have fun writing that!

PUER: But you see, the hero's little sister has tracked the captives to the sacred mistletoe hedge near the underground palace. All alone, in the mysterious deep forest she has hidden, tele-kinetically deprogramming the extraterrestrial's computer. Then, after waiting and watching long, she furtively enters the mushroom where all these adolescent boys are bound. Almost in a trance she unbinds them, using the magical scythe she has found under the deformed mandragora!

BEATRICE: [*Touched in spite of himself*] God, I wish you had been reviewing for the major publications when it was published. None of the critics could follow it...

PUER: I thought the implication of that scene was that in facing the future we are all bound, paralyzed until we can discover the sweet feminine inside ourselves to free us. [BEATRICE *has started to cry*] Why are you crying?

BEATRICE: [*Denying his emotion*] Did you escape from some booby hatch?

PUER: You intended none of that? In a way it was that novel and your books of poems that brought me here. In the novel there is silliness and suffering; and a playful girl becomes a heroine laughing, because she can embrace the sufferings of others. You see, in the home we were taught during the day that we must short circuit all feelings and repress any sympathy we might have for the miseries of ordinary humans. Not only were we not to mythologize them as you have done, we were to mock them. We were taught during the day that in doing this we would escape all pain. But pain, so it seemed to me, is the twin of consciousness, and it is consciousness that makes us human. Perhaps consciousness is a disease but if so, it is a divine disease. We must seek to spread it...

BEATRICE: You make me feel like a fool; an unfeeling fool. I've forgotten how to respond naturally. I seem to camp automatically now, to expect insincerity, and admire finely wrought falsehood, and I shrug off everything. How can *I*—this dung heap of failed aspirations—have fathered something like you? Where am I in you? I don't love you and I feel so guilty. I have nothing to give you. Please, please, go away and I'm sorry ... [*He turns away from* PUER *to bite back his tears.*]

PUER: But... [*The door opens.* PASQUALE, DANNY *and* PATRICIA *stand there, threateningly.*]

PATRICIA: [*Entering*] Go off to the opera, Puer, there's an early curtain tonight. [PUER *looks from them to* BEATRICE, *undecided.*]

BEATRICE: [*Firmly*] Go ahead.

PASQUALE: [*To* PUER*f*] Here's a fifty for the taxi—[*Hands* PUER *money as he leaves. Then he turns to* BEATRICE.] How are you Bucky? My sister says she brought you a phone.

DANNY: Yeah, I installed it.

PASQUALE: [*Looking around, with false bonhomie*] When you going to furnish this place?

BEATRICE: What do you want, Pasquale?

PASQUALE: [*Settling down magisterially in the armchair*] Some wine might be nice. I got a wully [*This is South Philly slang for a craving*] for some fresh bread with wine.

BEATRICE: [*Sarcastic*] Why don't you go to church?

PASQUALE: But ain't this a church, Bucky? A temple of art?

BEATRICE: What happened to the good old-fashioned Mafia when you guys came in with a hammer and piano wire and left irony to the sentencing judge? [PATRICIA *shifts nervously.*]

PASQUALE: It's nice bantering with you, Bucky, but my sister's standin' there making buttons. Look, it's simple; you got to move back in with her.

BEATRICE: Why?

PASQUALE: She's runnin' for Congress in six months.

BEATRICE: Good for her.

PASQUALE: But you see, Bucky, this is America...

DANNY: The free world...

PASQUALE: And in America you can't run for higher office with a fag for a husband.

DANNY: It's better than in Russia where you can't run for higher office at all...

PASQUALE: Right.

BEATRICE: But our divorce will be final by then...

PATRICIA: Oh come on, Beatrice, it's a Catholic District, you can't expect them to elect a recently divorced woman...

PASQUALE: Especially since she plans to run on the Family First platform ... And we figure it for a rough fight, her opposition...

DANNY: I spit on him ... [*Spits*]

PASQUALE: Will do as much damage as he can.

BEATRICE: I understand. But I have a reputation...

DANNY: Those bars are closed.

BEATRICE: No, I mean a literary reputation! I'm not sure America thinks the author of *Little Boy Bound* is a straight arrow.

PASQUALE: America don't think any writer is a straight arrow but America don't read...

DANNY: Television has made us a sub-literate population ... [*To* PASQUALE *and* PATRICIA *who are annoyed at his interruptions.*] It's true, it ain't my fault.

PASQUALE: And America thinks what the media tells it to think. We own quite a bit of this media and anyway your *Little Boy Bound* was a success how many years ago? None of your other stuff got taken serious outside of a few literary magazines...

DANNY: Don't feel bad, Beatrice, I read some of it!

PASQUALE: [*Annoyed*] Yo!

DANNY: Sorry.

PASQUALE: So, look, my papa...

DANNY: Cumbar' Antonio...

PASQUALE: He knows, you idiot, he grew up around the corner!

DANNY: Oh, right...

PASQUALE: [*Continuing, to* BEATRICE] So my papa wants you to move back in with baby sister here. If you're good you can go to Puerto Rico and play with the boys there in a year or so.

BEATRICE: I did not move here to play with the boys as you put it.

I came here to try and grow up. I'm thirty-six and I want to be on my own...

PASQUALE: And this kid living here?

PATRICIA: We know all about him. He even got a job at McDonald's. What do you call him, your Chicken McNugget?

BEATRICE: That kid is here temporarily, and we're not having sex!

PASQUALE: Look, Bucky, I ain't got nothin' against fags...

DANNY: Some of my best friends are fags...

PASQUALE: My best bookie is a fag...

DANNY: And don't forget Father O'Donnell...

PASQUALE: Now he's a fag and we let him pray for us. So I'm not bein' ... what is that word...

DANNY: Sexist.

PASQUALE: Sexist. I mean, far as we're concerned you can stick your dick anywheres you want...

DANNY: Except in the ravioli right before we eat it ... [PASQUALE *glares*] Just a joke.

PASQUALE: My point is we don't want the world to know. You're one of us by marriage to my sister. So move back in with her, can the divorce, and there won't be any trouble.

PATRICIA: Please, Beatrice. [BEATRICE *thinks for a minute then pulls* PATRICIA *into a mock foxtrot while singing:*]

BEATRICE: [*Sings and dances*] "It seems we've stood and talked like this, before..." Remember, Patricia? Two years ago it was because it would look bad at your practice. The year before that it was because it would coincide with the anniversary of Cumbar' Antonio's first hit...

PATRICIA: [*Impatient*] Silver Jubilee...

DANNY: He was hitting people long before his wedding.

BEATRICE: And before that it was because of my third novel and I couldn't face the stress and before that ... But why go on? If I come back now it will mean I can never leave, whether you win or lose this election, or even actually run. There'll always be another election or family celebration. There may be no more novels of course—not a tragedy for you or the American reading public or posterity if any—but a catastrophe for me. So my answer is no! [*The two Mafiosi and* PATRICIA *tense.* BEATRICE *turns to* PASQUALE *who is looking more menacing by the second.*] You're her brother, Pasquale, persuade her to find some normal man who'll give her children before it's too late and who can love her as a husband loves a wife. You do her that favor, persuade your father to do her that favor, but leave me alone. And I'm sorry if our problems affect the election...

PASQUALE: Now, of course, if she was a widow, that would be all right...

DANNY: He means if you died right now, Beatrice...

PATRICIA: [*Upset*] I'm leaving. Look, Beatrice you're going to have to come back, like it or not. Your son can stay with me if you need him to, nothing will be taken out on him. But if you don't come back there's going to be real trouble. [*Leaves*] [PASQUALE *glares at* BEATRICE *trying to terrify him.* BEATRICE *becomes a little nervous since even* DANNY *suddenly looks hard and furthermore is blocking the door.* BEATRICE *determines to stand up to* PASQUALE *but edges a little toward the windows just in case.*]

BEATRICE: [*To* PASQUALE] Look, I don't want any trouble but I'm not afraid. And why can't you understand this marriage is wrong—wrong for me, wrong for her...

PASQUALE: If something is wrong that's up to God and Cumbar' Antonio to decide. [PASQUALE *slowly puts on his leather gloves—the kind that don't leave marks after a beating.*]

BEATRICE: [*Trying to stand his ground while edging further toward the window.*] I wasn't afraid of you, Squeegie...

PASQUALE: [*Stung*] Don't call me that...

BEATRICE: [*Getting closer to the windows*] I wasn't afraid of you when you were the terror of Snyder Avenue, had so much acne you looked like one big pimple and so much body odor we called your smell the early warning system. And now that you're a heavy investor in Clearasil, and immerse yourself daily in ten gallons of cheap cologne and cheat on your income taxes like the most respectable white collar criminal I find you even less scary!

DANNY: [*Impressed*] Boy, these writers can really sling the invective. [*Puts on his leather gloves*]

PASQUALE: You mean these perverts!

BEATRICE: And I'll break your head if you come anywhere near me! [*Runs for the windows, opens one and with an agility born of terror, more or less leaps out onto the fire escape.* PASQUALE *looks at* DANNY, *they both laugh.*]

PASQUALE: Funny what a bunch of leather gloves bought on sale at Alexander's can do—they can turn a chubby writer into a circus monkey...

DANNY: These writers can really leap around... [*They both laugh heartily.*]

PASQUALE: Hey, Bucky, come back in. We ain't gonna do nothin' today!

BEATRICE: [*A little abashed, peeking through the window.*] You sure? [*He climbs back*] Well—I meant what I said.

PASQUALE: I'm sure you did, Bucky, I'm not gonna get into a hissy fight with you. I bet you're a real menace with them nails. I gotta family now anyway, so I don't get into fights unless I'm forced, and it takes a real man to force me, not a bunch of words. And I don't hold grudges, ain't profitable in the real world. My papa gave me a job to do for the good of the family and I gotta do it. I ain't lookin' to hurt nobody, but I will if I have to, and you ain't the only vulnerable human around, you certainly ain't the youngest.

BEATRICE: What are you talking about? Those kids...

PASQUALE: You just start packin'—one way or the other you're movin' back in with my sister.

DANNY: He means it, Beatrice.

PASQUALE: Yo! Danny—catch up with my sister, make sure she's okay.

DANNY: Yo! [*Leaves*]

PASQUALE: [*Makes a slow and grand exit to the door, pauses in the doorway and turns to face* BEATRICE.] And I ain't had a pimple in seventeen years! [*Out.* BEATRICE, *badly frightened and realizing that both* DY *and* PUER *are in jeopardy, is left alone. He paces. Then he remembers he has a phone now. He picks up the receiver and dials.*]

BEATRICE: [*On the phone*] Hi—is this Terry—this isn't the William Morris Agency? Sorry. [*Hangs up, dials again, waits trying to control his panic.*] Hi, is this Terry? This is Bart. [*Pause*] Bartholemew Dante. I know its been a while. Look, is George there? No, I'd rather wait, it's real important. Thanks. [*Waits, paces*] Hi, George, thanks for taking the call ... I know, long time no speak. [*Listens*] I'm still trying to get started but I was wondering—look George, I'm in a jam, I'm broke and I may need to get out of town—you know my wife's family—yes, well, what I told you might happen has happened, they're making trouble. No, wait George, I've got to talk to you—I'll hold. [*He waits*] Oh hi ... isn't it pilot season? Remember you said you'd pitch that pilot idea of mine at CBS? You remember—*Mother Trigger.* Yes, *Mother Trigger*—you know, it's about the Mother Superior in the Old West who is the only survivor of a wagon train massacre on the way to California? Yes, and she travels around with her rosaries and her six-guns saving the innocent and killing the damned? Well, she has a club foot—that makes her sympathetic. Yes, in the pilot she guns down the seven desperados bent on rape, teaches the deaf dumb hermaphrodite to sign and be self-accepting, sings the "Ave Maria" at the old maid's wedding which she has arranged, then limps off into the sunset to convert the local Iroquois. [*Listens*] I know it sounds campy but they don't produce *Hamlet* after all. [*Listens*] No, I don't own a TV. Watch it? Oh, you mean watch it as a source of ideas—no, I guess that does make sense. [*Listens*] No, okay, we'll speak soon; have lunch, sure. [*Hangs up*] Fucking phones! [*Kicks the phone across the floor.* DY *enters with armfulls of bags from McDonald's.*]

DY: Hi. I passed your ex-wife—she was getting into a car with these two fierce-looking creeps.

BEATRICE: [*Concerned*] They didn't see you?

DY: No, I was able to duck under this umbrella ... I borrowed it at work. She looked kind of sad, you know? Anyway, I brought us supper—I told you I'd bring back a surprise. I get kinda tired of Sarah Lee and Haagen-Dazs.

BEATRICE: Thanks. [*They organize to have dinner.* BEATRICE *starts taking out the food,* DY *gets a few plates and sets up a box as a table.*]

DY: I also got some wine. I thought white would go better with Chicken McNuggets than red. The clerk in the liquor store said I was cute and gave me a discount and also sold me this bhang. He said like the wine was great for it. [*Holds up an enormous, peculiar looking bhang.*] And he gave me this ... [*Holds up a nickel bag of dope.*]

BEATRICE: Oh, I don't smoke dope.

DY: You don't? Like, why?

BEATRICE: Everybody I know is either a junkie or a born-again

Christian and it all started with smoking dope. [*Opening a carton*] What are these?

DY: Pickled eggs.

BEATRICE: At McDonald's?

DY: Well, it's Soho, you know. [DY *gets some glasses and they settle down around the improvised table to eat.*]

BEATRICE: [*Eating*] It's not too bad.

DY: [*Eating*] Sometimes it's like sobering to realize that like half the world eats this food; but then, I realize I eat it too. [DY *pours* BEATRICE *some wine; they drink.*]

BEATRICE: Have you thought of calling your parents? I have a phone now.

DY: Oh yeah? Where?

BEATRICE: [*Pointing*] I kicked it over there.

DY: Neat.

BEATRICE: Patricia and friend installed it.

DY: Wow.

BEATRICE: So will you call your parents?

DY: Why?

BEATRICE: I'm sure they're worried silly. It's been awhile...

DY: Not that long. And if I called them from here they'd try and trace the call, I know them. Look, if like you don't want me to stay any longer, I'll move out and not be angry with you either. You've been great to me. But I'm never going back there. Have some more wine. [DY *pours, they eat and drink.*]

BEATRICE: Thanks ... I'm glad you brought this stuff ... Look, I like you Dy, and there's no problem with your staying here a little longer as far as I'm concerned. But my ex-wife is getting desperate and her family is getting crazy. They're dangerous people...

DY: I'll stick by you Beatrice, I mean it. You haven't had many friends in your life. I haven't either but I think I have a better idea of friendship than you do. I'll stick by you, fight for you if I have to. And I'm *mean*—I subscribe to *Soldier of Fortune,* remember.

BEATRICE: [*Smiling in spite of himself*] Okay, okay, I guess you're safe enough for a few days; anyway, I hope so. How's the job?

DY: Oh, great. Mr. Acquierro—he's like the manager and all; he says he thinks I have a big future in corporate management.

BEATRICE: But what do you *do*?

DY: Well, for example, like today, members of the Community Board came by. And Mr. Acquierro brought them over to see me, standing there smiling. And like, I made conversation with them and told them how great it was of them to like let McDonald's build in Soho and hire young people and provide cheap but nutritious meals for the underprivileged and all.

BEATRICE: And they didn't throw up all over you?

DY: No, though a few of them like laughed a little. Like, have some more wine. [*Pours for both of them*] But they like loved me. One man, who said he was a lawyer asked for my phone number, and this nice old man told me he had a great French chef on his yacht and I was welcome to come aboard any time, and this young man, well sort of young, I think, asked if he could sketch me—in saran wrap! Mr. Acquierro was thrilled. So, naturally I was feeling very good about myself so I like sauntered over to this babe in shorts and I paused, then said: "Like, hi." And she said: "Drop dead!" Well, I paused for reflection. And then, about twenty minutes later, this real neat girl like smiled at me and I like smiled back then she like flared her nostrils, so I like flared my nostrils, then she opened her mouth wide and showed me her braces and I thought she looked cute with them so I opened my mouth wide and showed her my slight overbite and she yawned! I mean it, she yawned! So I like checked my breath and pits; they were okay and then I asked her what was wrong. And you know what she said?

BEATRICE: "I'm a transsexual and am feeling tender today?"

DY: No, like listen! I'm serious! She said I wasn't funky!

BEATRICE: Oh.

DY: What's that mean?

BEATRICE: Have some wine, Dy. [*Pours them both wine*] Well, how can I put it. You see Dy, you're white bread.

DY: I'm what?

BEATRICE: White bread.

DY: [*Horrified*] Nobody has ever called me white bread before. An Anglo Swine, yes, but white bread, never! We don't even eat white bread at home. Mom serves onion rolls and bagels, never white bread!

BEATRICE: Don't get upset—it's not fatal. But you're not funky.

DY: I have to get my notebook! [*Does so*] Now, be brutal. What tells you I'm not funky?

BEATRICE: At a distance in the dark?

DY: [*Forcing himself to be brave.*] Yes.

BEATRICE: [*Thinks: half serious*] Your walk.

DY: [*Stung*] What's wrong with my walk?

BEATRICE: It's a WASP shimmy. You walk more or less like this. [*he walks more or less like* DY, *teasingly exaggerating so that indeed the walk resembles a tight-arsed shimmy.*] Now, somebody funky, somebody from South Philly, for example, walks like this. [*No more seriously,* BEATRICE *walks like the greasers of his childhood.*] See, somebody walking like this is aware of his balls intersecting with the law of gravity! [*Walking up a storm*] Oh those balls are clanking and rumbling, making music. There! [*He settles down and drinks some more wine, aware that he's becoming quite tipsy.* DY *writes earnestly in his notebook, takes a few sips of wine, then stands up.*]

DY: [*With the utmost seriousness*] All right, watch. I'm going to walk funky! [DY, *fueled by the wine, attempts an imitation of* BEATRICE, *trying very hard to walk funky.*] What do you think?

BEATRICE: That's like a spastic. Watch closer! [BEATRICE *walks again.* DY *watches with intense concentration.*]

DY: [*Imitating* BEATRICE] This is hard! Why didn't my parents raise me to walk funky? [*Tries very hard,* BEATRICE *suppresses a giggle and swallows some more wine.* DY *works very hard at his walk and starts to improve.*] Now, wait, I think I'm getting it. These are the muscles I use in tennis.

BEATRICE: [*Can't resist teasing* DY] Well, a few more years ... [DY *looks stung*] No, no, that was much better.

DY: [*Drinks more wine*] But keep coaching me. I need to learn this stuff.

BEATRICE: Now Dy, don't you think I'm an exotic choice for a tutor in heterosexuality?

DY: But you used to be straight, my father never talks to me, my brother hates me, who am I going to learn from? Besides, if *I'm* not funky believe me nobody in my family is! I'd teach you to be a WASP if you wanted! Come on—I learn fast. See? [*Walks funky, more fluently than before.*] How'm I doing?

BEATRICE: [*Drinks some wine and watches critically.*] Better, but something's missing.

DY: What? [*A little out of breath, he drinks some wine. By this time both are tipsy.*]

BEATRICE: It's not just the walk, it's the talk. Somebody funky says the right sort of think; like, [*In a funky manner*] "Hi, doll!"

DY: [*Imitating*] "Hi, doll!"

BEATRICE: Be careful of that accent. I want a South Philly "O". [BEATRICE *strikes an elaborate funky pose, then says his phrase with delectation.*] "Hi, doll!"

DY: [*Imitates pose and phrase*] "Hi, doll!"

BEATRICE: [*Goes further with posing and accent*] "Yo! Let's go get a piece a' pizza!" [*Since he is exaggerating, this phrase sounds something like: "Yoeu! Leutz goue geh-ah beece-ah beetz!"*]

DY: [*Doing his best*] "Yo! Let's go get a piece a' pizza!"

BEATRICE: Listen more carefully! [*After taking a swig of wine*] "Yo! Let's go get a piece a' pizza!"

DY: [*With determination*] Okay! [*Prepares himself with a swig of wine, then gets into character. He strikes a funky pose, takes a funky walk around the room, strikes another funky pose as though having seen a beautiful vision, and says as though with a steel tongue in a mouth of cotton wool.*] "Hi, doll. Let's go get a piece a' pizza!"

BEATRICE: [*Striking the corresponding feminine pose*] "No thank you, I have to go study my Geology."

DY: [*Surprised*] What?

BEATRICE: [*Himself*] I'm playing along, be serious! [*Strikes feminine pose, says in South Philly accent*] "No thank you, I have to study my Geology!"

DY: Uh ... uh ... what should I say? [BEATRICE *impatiently rolls his eyes*] I'm funky, I'm funky, be patient!

BEATRICE: [*As doll, miming elaborate impatience*] "My Geology book is getting lonesome."

DY: [*Strikes funky pose, saunters over to* BEATRICE *funkily and accosts the doll.*] "I got all the rocks you'll ever need, babe." [*Drunk by now, laughs riotously thinking this hilarious.*]

BEATRICE: [*As doll, smirking*] "I'm not studying rocks for your information, I'm into fossils; fossilization is my life's ambition."

DY: [*As funky dude*] "You're far out, babe, let's go to the prom!"

[*Pulls* BEATRICE *into a wild disco dance.* BEATRICE *by now also drunk goes along and soon they are stamping around crazily. Soon both are out of breath and laughing uproariously. They slow down and split the last of the wine.*] What was your prom's theme?

BEATRICE: The Catholic Life Force! The girls put blue everywhere and had babies on top of everything. It was fab—that was our word for great!

DY: [*Still moving around*] Fab! Dance with me!

BEATRICE: [*Starting to move also; both are moving slowly as the wine works.*] Which dance?

DY: Which dance?

BEATRICE: Well, there was the Fish, there was the Monkey, then there was the Watusi, the Shimmy, the Frug, the Locomotion, the Bugaloo and the old people, they did the Twist.

DY: Oh, I mean slow dancing. [*Starts weaving about*]

BEATRICE: [*Surprised*] Slow dancing?

DY: My mom always said that was the most romantic. That jumping around, it's the same as kids my age do. [*He is more or less slow dancing alone.*] Come on—teach me to funky slow dance. Let's sing something and dance.

BEATRICE: [*Feeling his way, not exactly sure what all this portends*] What should we sing?

DY: [*Holds his arms out, dancing*] Something we both know.

BEATRICE: You don't know *Tristan Und Isolde* by any chance? No? Let me see, some Cole Porter?

DY: [*Having never heard of him*] He's good. Sing something!

BEATRICE: Well, here goes. Better let me lead and I have big feet so watch out! Oops—gotta pray first. [*Makes* DY *cross himself*] Holy Mary Mother of God forgive my sentimentality. [*Sings softly*] "You'd be so easy to love, so easy to idolize all others above, so worth the yearning for, so swell to keep all the home fires burning for..." [*They dance. At first* BEATRICE *clowns at little, singing and hamming, keeping* DY *at arm's length.* DY *is intent on learning the steps and after a while starts humming along, approximating the tune. Both are drunk, the loft is shadowy and it is raining out.* BEATRICE *feels the mood as romantic and surrenders to it.* DY *closes his eyes also feeling this mood. soon they are dancing close and tenderly.* DY *stiffens for a second then yields, carried away by the warmth and the wine as much as anything.* BEATRICE *realizes at this moment he can push this into something overtly sexual. He is tempted ... his own loneliness, his fear, the desperate situation he is in draw him toward* DY *as much as the attraction he has always felt for him, and has so far denied. He stops humming, thinking.* DY *continues humming the song and rather sleepily presses into* BEATRICE. BEATRICE *kisses* DY's *forehead and disengages himself.*]

DY: [*Surprised at this abrupt movement.*] What's the matter?

BEATRICE: You're too drunk and I'm not drunk enough. In any case the morning and McDonald's beckons.

DY: [*Dances in place, smiling, tipsy*] That was nice.

BEATRICE: Niceness like that, sadly, is one of life's nastier traps ... Good night!

DY: Yeah—I have to get up early tomorrow ... [*But he still dances in place, smiling.* BEATRICE *starts cleaning up, retrieving the McDonald's cartons, the wine bottle and the other utensils they have used. After a while* DY *undresses for bed, pulls the bed closer to the radiator.* BEATRICE *has been going in and out of the room.* DY *gets into bed. He smiles up at* BEATRICE.] Sit down for a second?

BEATRICE: You should go to sleep.

DY: I am, I am, but sit down a second. [BEATRICE *sits down on the bed.* DY *snuggles up to him.*]

BEATRICE: You'll have a stiff neck in the morning...

DY: Just stay until I'm asleep ... Put some music on?

BEATRICE: Some pop?

DY: Whatever you like.

BEATRICE: You got it, Mahler: He's good for renunciation. [BEATRICE *gets up and puts on a tape of* The Song of the Earth—*the last movement, "The Farewell."* BEATRICE *smiles at the irony and sits down again on the bed. Soon* DY *is asleep, lulled by the soft, sad music.* BEATRICE *stares down at him, fully experiencing the longing he has repressed. He tucks* DY *in, then stands up. There is a soft knock at the door.* BEATRICE *opens it.* PUER *stands there looking miserable.*]

PUER: Please, may I stay with you tonight? Patricia has been kind but she is your enemy and I fear I may be used against you. But if you like I will sleep outside...

BEATRICE: No, I have a sleeping bag ... [BEATRICE *goes into another room and returns with a sleeping bag.* PUER *gets into it.*]

PUER: Thank you.

BEATRICE: Good night. [*He turns the lights off and walks into his bedroom.* PUER *sits up and looks toward the sleeping* DY.]

CURTAIN. END ACT TWO

ACT THREE

Scene One

[BEATRICE'*s loft, a week later. Morning. For once bright light streams through* BEATRICE'*s windows. Now, however, they are barred in typical New York City fashion.* BEATRICE *has further unpacked; and odds and ends of his former life can be seen placed at random around the loft. These consist mostly of elaborate old-fashioned religious statues collected by* BEATRICE *as a camp. There are also some sloppily installed bookcases filled mainly with paperbacks, and shelves for records and tapes. A mass of complicated and sophisticated-looking computer equipment occupies one corner of the room. This has been assembled by* PUER. *Otherwise,* BEATRICE *is still writing on a sturdy box—his beat-up typewriter is there; and there is more paper—*BEATRICE *seems to have been working less fitfully.* DY *is asleep on the rollaway bed.* PUER'*s sleeping bag, located near the computer equipment, is empty.* BEATRICE *appears in once-elegant, now faded and poorly maintained pajamas and robe. He is wearing much abused tennis shoes as slippers. He is carrying a diet Pepsi, and sipping it drowsily. He stares for a second at the sleeping* DY, *then checks* PUER'*s sleeping bag and starts folding it. After a time he sits on the rollaway bed and with great affection touches* DY'*s head.* DY *mumbles and turns over.* BEATRICE *lifts up the bottom end of the quilt and tickles a bare foot.* DY *starts awake. He sees* BEATRICE *and smiles, cuddling up to him.*]

DY: [*Still sleepy*] Like, good morning.

BEATRICE: No like about it and I think you may be late for work.

DY: [*Yawns*] it doesn't really matter. I'm in management training. [*Sees the diet Pepsi in* BEATRICE'*s hand.*] Beatrice, you're killing yourself! A diet Pepsi already?

BEATRICE: Carbonation and additives make many a morning bearable.

DY: [*Looks toward sleeping bag*] Where's Puer?

BEATRICE: He left on some mysterious mission as I awoke.

DY: [*Cuddles easily in* BEATRICE'*s arms*] I'd love to go back to sleep.

BEATRICE: [*Quoting*] "Time's winged chariot and so on and so on..."

DY: Oh, like that's a quote from what's-his-name—we read him in...

BEATRICE: [*Sardonic*] Antiquated Forms Seminar!

DY: Right! [*Jumps up on the rollaway, arranges the blanket around him and playfully declaims:*] "Had we but world enough and time, this coyness, lady, would be no crime..." And so on ... And remember this? [*He strikes another quasi-heroic pose and quotes:*] "But at my back I always hear Time's winged chariot hurrying near..."

BEATRICE: [*Also strikes pose and quotes:*] "And yonder all before us lie deserts of vast eternity!" And speaking of vast deserts, McDonald's beckons!

DY: Okay! [BEATRICE *has playfully tackled* DY *who mock tussles with him for a moment then lays comfortably in* BEATRICE's *arms.*] You know, its been great this past week, even with Puer here. I mean, you're weird by St. Paul's standards—these religious statues for instance! If my mother could only see them!

BEATRICE: [*Mock shudders*] Jesus Forfend!

DY: But buying a few of them that day with you on Fourteenth Street, that was—well like fab! And just being with you ... oh shit, I'm chattering like a goon, but I've never had a friend like you, never!

BEATRICE: Me neither.

DY: Look what I wrote in my notebook about you. [*Reaches for his notebook under his pillow.*]

BEATRICE: You sleep with your writing?

DY: Keeps me warm! And you know when you wake up in the middle of the night with ideas?

BEATRICE: I used to know...

DY: Well, it's good to have it handy, now listen! [*He finds a place in his notebook and reads.*] "I saw Beatrice last night flickering in the strange rain light of Prince Street, laughing, tossing his head like crazy Ezra Hopkins in the *Bacchae*" [*Explains to* BEATRICE] Like, I was in the *Bacchae* in ninth grade...

BEATRICE: The *Bacchae* in prep school?

DY: Oh, it was rad, and like Ezra played the mother who eats her son and he tossed his head a lot like you, but listen! [*Reads some more*] "Then, suddenly, he stood still and seemed huge to me. In that light he seemed a man/woman; an ancient sorcerer; he even weaves spells with his diet Pepsi..."

BEATRICE: [*Touched and charmed by this*] Well you certainly have a vivid imagination and you have to get up! Now!

DY: [*Getting out of bed*] I wonder where Puer got to?

BEATRICE: [*Wistfully*] Maybe he stowed away back to Germany.

DY: [*Thinks about this, rejects it*] No, he left all his gear. I like him. I feel sorry you don't.

BEATRICE: You do?

DY: Oh shit, Beatrice, who am I to take a moral tone with you? I don't know anything about anything ... but you know—my father isn't crazy about me either. Like you ought to hug Puer once in awhile—force yourself. He needs it ... What time is it? [*Finds the clock*] Oh shit! Why didn't you wake me up? I don't have time to jog or have breakfast. I'll take a shower...

BEATRICE: That's all?

DY: I can munch out on McMuffins at work! [*Races off to take a shower*]

BEATRICE: [*Alone*] McMuffins at work?! [*As in the Italian opera*] Io tremo! [*With trepidation he approaches his typewriter. He glances over some of his recent work and shudders. He waves his can of diet Pepsi over the typewriter, sorcerer-like.*] I'm weaving a spell over you, oh keyboard. Guide my fingers to the words, come on, guide them ... [*Nothing happens*] Well, so much for his accuracy! [*Settles down to work, types desultorily for a moment. There is a knock at the door.*] There's nobody home!

DANNY: [*Outside*] Yo, Beatrice, open up, it's me!

BEATRICE: Yo, Danny! [*Takes some time opening the door because he has added an elaborate lock*] You're alone?

DANNY: [*Entering*] yeah, I'm on my way to work. Where are the kids?

BEATRICE: One is at his matutinal libations, the other at a place unknown.

DANNY: [*Seeing the computer*] Look at all this stuff! Where'd you get it?

BEATRICE: Puer got it. He hit every computer store in town and bet the head salesman he could solve any puzzle or win any game. He was thrown out of thirty, they called the police at seven—luckily or unluckily he has an American passport so all they could do was complain to the salesmen—but at the others they took him up on it. He won all this. He's already had about ten offers to join the sales force at these places. And the owner of the biggest place gave him a hundred dollars to leave and never come back. It's terrifying. You'd think after all those years of doing my Easter Duty, some saint at least would have appeared to warn me away from Henrietta's loins. But she worked an awful fascination and I succumbed without warnings or omens.

DANNY: [*Looking over the equipment*] Is he invading government files?

BEATRICE: I hope not. What if they got a search warrant and found my porn collection? Think of the embarrassment! Think of the expense of trying to replace all those out-of-print magazines—porn is like Grand Opera, it just isn't what it used to be! You want some breakfast?

DANNY: Sure, I could go for some cake and ice cream. You got coke?

BEATRICE: As in the soft drink?

DANNY: What do you think? I'm respectable and working class, we don't sniff shit.

BEATRICE: [*Calling off*] Dy? Can Danny have some of your coke?

DY: [*Off*] Sure!

BEATRICE: It's lucky these kids are self-supporting. I'll be back with breakfast! [*Exits into the kitchen.* DY *re-enters from his shower more or less dressed.*]

DY: [*Sees* DANNY, *joking but wary*] Have you come to kills us?

DANNY: Yo, wise guy! Show some respect! You should go back to Gardenpartyville.

DY: Oh, fuck you!

DANNY: Fuck me? Fuck me?

DY: Yeah, you heard me, like fuck you!

DANNY: Say that again. I dare you, say that again.

DY: Fuck you. Double fuck you. Quadruple fuck you. Fuck fuck fuck fuck fuck fuck you!

DANNY: Let me get this straight. Fuck me?

DY: Yeah! [*Suddenly they spring at one another and tussle, crashing into things.* BEATRICE *appears with the breakfast tray*

*and emits a piercing and long scream, which separates the
boys.*]

BEATRICE: [*Impressed with the noise he has made*] All those
years in the all male opera must have paid off. I think that was
more or less a high "C". So my adolescent guests are on
maneuvers?

DANNY: This little Anglo Swine gave me lip!

DY: You greasy Wop! [*They begin to fight again,* BEATRICE *stops
them.*]

BEATRICE: Please, it's too early for ethnic epithets. Aren't you
late for work, Dy?

DY: Yes. I'm sorry Beatrice. [*Turns to* DANNY] As for you...!

BEATRICE: [*Pushing him toward the door*] Yo! McDonald's calls!

DY: Yo! [*Leaves.* BEATRICE *relocks the door. Then returns to*
DANNY *and breakfast. He notices* DANNY *is upset.*]

BEATRICE: What's the matter?

DANNY: I couldn't even take that milk toast white asshole!

BEATRICE: So you're not a morning person. You'd have taken
him in a trice at midnight.

DANNY: [*Comforted*] You think so?

BEATRICE: Is the Pope a Polish transvestite? [*Having poured
Coke for* DANNY] Now, to what do I owe this visit?

DANNY: Look, Beatrice, it ain't my place to say it and I'm taking
a risk, but you better be careful. I think you're in love with that
kid.

BEATRICE: Is it that obvious?

DANNY: yeah. You looked at me like that once.

BEATRICE: Oh no, I didn't.

DANNY: Yes, it was at the Columbus Day Picnic in South Philly.
You was back for the day and famous then. I was the shortstop
in the softball game—you remember—between the St. Monica's
altar boys and choir boys?

BEATRICE: [*Having forgotten*] Oh yes...

DANNY: I made the winning run but scraped my knee real bad.
You remember? You ran for the mercurochrome, then kissed
the cut. I was real proud even though everybody said you was
a fairy.

BEATRICE: You're making me nostalgic. [*He's been serving the
Haagen-Dazs ice cream, now he starts on the Sarah Lee
chocolate pound cake, which is frozen solid. As he and* DANNY

talk he gets a hammer and a sharp knife and hammers the knife into the cake, excavating slices for himself and DANNY.]
DANNY: So look, Cumbar' Antonio and Pasquale and Patricia have something planned. I might have to do somethin' and it won't be anything personal. It's my job but it makes me feel bad.
BEATRICE: Maybe you should quit.
DANNY: What would my mother and brothers say? And if I fuck up this assignment with Pasquale they're gonna make me join the police force and work from inside and I hate that! [*They eat their ice cream and cake for a minute, pensively.*] After you kissed the cut that day I sorta hung around you. I kept expectin' you to make a pass...
BEATRICE: You sound disappointed.
DANNY: Well, maybe.
BEATRICE: I thought you were straight.
DANNY: I am, I am, but I have aberrations.
BEATRICE: And aren't you getting married soon?
DANNY: To Maria Basiola!
BEATRICE: Oh, I know her, she's terrific.
DANNY: Look, Beatrice, you're good people, I don't think nothin' bad of you. I'm late, I better go. I don't want to join the Police Force, I couldn't stand that, so if they order me to do something...
BEATRICE: Should I run away? I'm broke. If I go somewhere nearby they'd just track me down. No, I've got to face this through. But thanks for the warning.
DANNY: Okay, Beatrice, but be careful. Last night at the crooked Bingo game Cumbar' Antonio gave his definition of an artist because he was thinkin' of you.
BEATRICE: I hesitate to ask what it was.
DANNY: He said: "An artist in Manhattan is no better than a sick shit in jaundice city."
BEATRICE: He always had a way with words. [*A rap at the door.* BEATRICE *and* DANNY *exchanges a worried look.*]
DANNY: [*Frightened*] It might be them! [*Another rap*]
BEATRICE: There's nobody here!
PUER: [*Outside*] Please, it is I.
BEATRICE: Alone or with others?
PUER: [*Outside*] Alone, naturally. [BEATRICE *opens the door.*

PUER *rollerskates in and poses. He has become an all-American city teenager overnight and with a vengeance. He is wearing a battered, poorly-fitted leather jacket, skin-tight tattered jeans and boots. He has had his hair done in a wild and woolly punk style—it now sticks up fearfully and riotously, erupting in all directions and displaying a full palette of garish colors.* BEATRICE *and* DANNY *stare at him, shocked. His huge dangling earrings—more of them than one could imagine his middle-sized ears supporting—are not lost on them; nor is his massive inked-on tattoo which is vague but looks indecent. In the doorway]* Like hi! [*He starts himself up and precariously rollerskates across the room and toward the bathroom door. He stops in the doorway and turns back.*] Like Anarchy now! [*Rollerskates out.* BEATRICE *and* DANNY *are left alone.*]

DANNY: [*To* BEATRICE, *in wonder*] That is the weirdest kid I've ever seen.

BEATRICE: I was thinking of giving him to you as a wedding present.

DANNY: No thanks. I'm late and Pasquale'll get suspicious. Shake my hand, Beatrice, just in case...

BEATRICE: Okay. [*They shake hands*]

DANNY: Yo! [*Leaves*]

BEATRICE: Yo!

PUER: [*Appearing from bathroom*] Yo! [BEATRICE *carefully locks door.*]

BEATRICE: Be careful who you let in here. And what happened?

PUER: I visited this *sehr charment* hair styling salon this morning. They adored me. I am anxious to become assimilated. Is not New York referred to as the great melting pot? I wish to be cooked tender in the great stew!

BEATRICE: Well, if you have to go into hiding, that's as good a disguise as any.

PUER: Oh, could my former schoolmates see me thus they would be orange with envy!

BEATRICE: Green is the color and I'm not sure it'd be envy.

PUER: [*Sits at the computer console*] And now sufficient idle chat. To work, my father, we must rescue your muse.

BEATRICE: What are we going to do?

PUER: Into this computer will we factor every element of the narrative of this new fiction of yours. Among other things, it

will then print out a thousand possible titles, some *natürlich*
more *outre* than others and we, my father, we will choose the
one likeliest to unfetter your recalcitrant muse.
BEATRICE: When will Henrietta be paroled?
PUER: Not in her lifetime, I'm afraid.
BEATRICE: [*As in the Italian opera*] Io Tremo! I feel like a fool
doing this!
PUER: But consider, my father, Balzac did not have a typewriter
﹨and thus might have said much the same thing...
BEATRICE: Now there's a thought! Balzac with a typewriter. He'd
have written fourteen or fifteen thousand more novels instead
of the six or seven hundred he managed by hand. Unless, of
course, we took away his coffee and made him write in the
morning. How did they do it? Those Old Masters who didn't
have central heating, indoor plumbing or electric light but who
wrote and wrote? *Why* did they do it? Was it because they
honestly thought their work mattered, that they were crucial to
their societies? Look at Dickens, or Tolstoy or Haydn or God
help us, Bach! What self-renewal they must have had! But they
were writing for their communities, or their God, for a world
they believed in need of them. Who am I writing for?
PUER: But when you were a success?
BEATRICE: I wasn't a success, I wasn't significant, I was a trend. I
was so ambitious in high school, I didn't realize all the ways
you could fail. There are as many circles in failure as there are
in hell. And listen to me run on, avoiding work. That's me,
Bartholemew Dante, aging chicken queen with logorrhea!
PUER: Chicken queen? Is that an idiom?
BEATRICE: Is it ever!
PUER: It means ... ach! I intuit the meaning. you love boys.
Have you ever investigated the possible roots of this amorous
taste?
BEATRICE: Well, Patricia paid for five years of psychoanalysis to
find out.
PUER: And...?
BEATRICE: The shrink...
PUER: I know that word, Dy had one too...
BEATRICE: ... went on and on about mother this and father that
and then I saw him being peed on by twelve men at the
Mineshaft one night, just ruining his leather—I realized then

where all the money Patricia paid him went. He was a strict Freudian.

PUER: Ah, yes, our professors had us read the fictions of Freud. They felt he and Proust were the only true great fabulists of the Twentieth Century.

BEATRICE: Freud and Proust?

PUER: Of course. They drew on similarly small circles of privileged eccentrics proud of, yet uneasy about their sexual proclivities, a similar obsession with the mother, even an analagous sense of sublimation through art.

BEATRICE: Well, I once knew an incestuous drag queen named Temps Perdu—maybe that's the Jungian archetype for the Proustian Freudian!

PUER: But are you not concerned about possible legal ramificatios in your pursuit of boys?

BEATRICE: For one thing I don't *pursue* boys: Sixteen is the youngest I've ever had and he was as big as I am and I was to find out just about as experienced sexually.

PUER: And I suspect, as with many a pederast, you are about to argue that with these young men you play the teacher, that there is even a positive value to the erotic contact.

BEATRICE: I was not about to argue that so we now know that mind reading is not one of your ten thousand talents. As it happens I am not sure any isolated sexual act has any major consequences for good or ill. Some of the young men did profit from contact with me because they were homosexuals and our great society persists in painting all homosexuals as miscreants and losers. They were relieved to meet a homosexual who was educated, clean, sane and friendly, able to function more or less in the day-to-day world and not immediately recognizable as a "Fag." As for the others, who knows? Some were just curious or horny. But if I haven't done a lot of good and am hardly about to recommend that we institutionalize adult/adolescent sex—and I emphasize *adolescent*—I'm not talking about children—I don't see I've done harm either. Even in the days before this awful AIDS thing I was careful and most of the time I indulged in what has come to be known as "safe sex." I have never thought that homo sexuality can be taught—certainly no one taught me and there are no serious statistical studies which indicate that either. One contact does not make a queer any more than one shot of whiskey makes a drunk or one moderately successful novel, two less successful novels and a couple of books of more or less pretentious and derivative poems makes a serious writer.

PUER: You are defensive, my father. But after all, boy love pre-exists the various narrow psuedo-Christian cults which preach against it and will probably survive them too, as human behavior of all sorts survives local strictures. Of course, humanity may not survive; and thus the moral problem will be solved neatly.

BEATRICE: Unless the roaches who survive us are into it.

PUER: Were you to ask me, I would speculate that you are attracted to boys—I am sorry, *adolescents,* and I believe it is more or less a fantasy you act on only occasionally for you could certainly have seduced Dy and have refrained from doing so, because you are in love with the potential you felt you had as a boy and are certain you, the adult, have lost. You sometimes bind them because you wish to bind that potential and control it. That is bizarre by the standards of the middle class worldwide, but not so incomprehensible yes?

BEATRICE: Why aren't you on television? They just love kids with all the answers. Maybe I should introduce you to my agent. If we got you a show that would solve all my financial problems.

PUER: You would have to acknowledge me as your son first.

BEATRICE: [*Defensive*] What do you mean? I've let you stay here. I even pawned *Death in Venice* so you'd have spending money.

PUER: You abhor me. I see it in your eyes. I have done what I could to interest you. This computer, my punk look they are all for you. They pain you. And I see the way you look at Dy, the way you hold him. That it is not sexual enrages me. I would like to kill him. [*He thinks*] That was jealousy, was it not? And hatred too. I have never felt those things before. How wonderful! I must tell Dy when he returns, he has acquainted me with a whole spectrum of my humanity! And now, refreshed by polite commerce, we must work.

BEATRICE: But look, if you feel like that maybe you should go back...

PUER: No more chat this morning, my father, we must not indulge ourselves too much. Work, work and more work, this must be our motto, personal problems later! [*Prepares com-*

puter]
BEATRICE: [*Watching with mixed emotions*] Oh, Virgin Mary, I know this is crazy but please let it help.
PUER: I am ready!
BEATRICE: All right, this titleless wonder I am trying to write is about this Italian-American...
PUER: [*Busy typing on the console*] Please describe him.
PUER: He's a sissy writer.
PUER: Ah! [*Makes adjustments on the console*] It is therefore autobiographical!
BEATRICE: No, he's talented!
PUER: Ah! [*Moves like mad around the computer*]
BEATRICE: [*Puzzled*] Ah?
PUER: I have just factored in your self-hatred! [DY's *voice is heard from offstage.*]
DY: [*Offstage, banging on the door*] Beatrice help!
BEATRICE: [*Unlocking the door, panicked*] Have they come for me?
DY: [*Rushing in, slamming the door behind him and locking it*] It's my brother, Trajan! He saw me at McDonald's. Hide me! He's right behind me! [*Rushes into the bathroom to hide.* TRAJAN MACDOWELL's *voice is heard outside the door.*]
TRAJAN'S VOICE: Dy?! Dy?! [*Knocks*] I know you're in there, Dy!
BEATRICE: What should I do?
PUER: I'll tell you! [*Factors all this into the computer*]
DY: [*Peeking out of the bathroom*] Don't let him find me!
TRAJAN: [*Offstage, knocking*] Come on, Dy!
PUER: [*Reading the advice the computer is printing out*] You should let him in, he may summon the police!
BEATRICE: [*Realizing the wisdom of this*] I'm sorry, Dy.
DY: Oh shit! [*Retreats into the bathroom.* BEATRICE *opens the door.* TRAJAN MACDOWELL *enters. He is a very preppy young man of nineteen, who enters out of breath but with considerable poise.*]
TRAJAN: [*To* BEATRICE] How do you do? I am Trajan MacDowell and I saw my little brother run in here...
DY: [*Opening the bathroom door in a fury.*] I'm *not* your little brother!
TRAJAN: [*Advancing determinately on* DY, *ignoring his tone*] Oh God, Dy, like I'm glad I found you, we've been going crazy!

DY: Stay out of my life! [*Suddenly* PATRICIA *and* PASQUALE *rush into the apartment.* PASQUALE *is wearing his gloves with a gun drawn.* DANNY *appears on the fire escape behind the barred window.*]

PASQUALE: [*Taking in all the boys*] What is this? A boy harem?

DANNY: [*Tugging at the bars*] Yo, Boss, I can't get in!

BEATRICE: Patricia, no...!

PATRICIA: You're in for it now!

PASQUALE: Kill them all!

TRAJAN: [*In horror, grabbing* DY] Help!

BLACKOUT
END SCENE ONE OF ACT THREE

Scene Two

[BEATRICE'*s loft, later that day.* DY, PUER, *and* TRAJAN *have been bound, hand and foot, they have also been gagged.* DANNY *has been left to stand guard, and is doing so rather indolently. Out of* BEATRICE'*s tape deck we hear Magda Olivero singing a hysterical outburst from Alfano's little known verisimo opera:* Risurrezione *(Resurrection, based on the Tolstoy novel).* DANNY *is pacing, listening impatiently and uncomprehendingly,* PUER *who has suggested this selection to distract him is making eye contact with the macho* DY *and the frankly terrified* TRAJAN. DY *is squirming in his bonds* Soldier of Fortune-*style, full of defiance.* TRAJAN *is frozen. Magda's outburst ends in a mad flurry of deafening sobs.* DANNY *is startled at first then switches off the tape deck in irritation.*]

DANNY: [*To* PUER] What the fuck is *wrong* with this chick? [*Removing* PUER'*s gag*] I thought you said this was gonna be "New Wave."

PUER: It is the opera *Risurrezione* by Alfano and that is the great Magda Olivero.

DANNY: What's she doin'? Throwin' a fuck?

PUER: She is lamenting the loss of her infant son, killed during a difficult birth in a snowstorm, the result of illicit sex with the Prince Dimitri! [DANNY *knits his brow trying to follow this.* DY

hurls himself up at DANNY, *of course losing his balance in the*
process and falling down.]
DANNY: [*To* DY] You're just gonna give yourself rope burns! [*To*
PUER] I don't trust you to tell me where Beatrice keeps his pop,
I bet he don't have any. So we're just gonna have to wait for
them in silence. [*Helping* DY *to stand up and hop to his chair.*]
Just be good and nobody'll get hurt.
PUER: [*Discreetly trying to loosen his bonds.*] My mother,
Henrietta the Terrorist, offered to train me in resisting ropes
the last time I saw her, but I laughed, unable to believe anyone
would want to bind me. Mothers often have foresight, have
they not? [DY *and* TRAJAN *make noises through their gags.*]
Danny, why don't you ungag them at least. They might choke.
DANNY: [*Thinks about it*] Well ... [*Ungags* DY *and* TRAJAN]
Don't bother callin' for help—this is New York City!
TRAJAN: [*Pathetically*] These are awfully tight, do you mind
loosening them?
DY: [*Macho*] Oh, Trajan, you're such a wimp!
TRAJAN: Hey, look, chill out! I didn't spend three days of my
break like trying to find you only to get tied up by some Mafia
Goon!
DANNY: I ain't no goon, you skinny wuss. I wish to hell they'd get
back here.
PUER: What are they going to do to my father?
TRAJAN: From the way they hustled him out of here I bet they're
going to like kill him!
PUER: No!
DANNY: No, Patricia loves him she doesn't want him dead. Of
course, Cumbar' Antonio and Pasquale—they're another story!
PUER: Where did they take him?
DANNY: To La Gioconda, this restaurant on Mulberry Street. It's
Cumbar' Antonio's favorite place. They're gonna have pig's
feet, clams and linguine and chocolate rum cannolis—that's
Cumbar' Antonio's Last Judgment Meal and then Beatrice is
gonna be given his choice of life with Patricia or death with
youse guys.
TRAJAN: Death with us? [*Struggles with his bonds*] Oh shit!
DY: I'm not afraid of death or torture!
TRAJAN: Oh great, your *Soldier of Fortune* number. I told dad
he should never have let you subscribe.

DY: If I ever get untied I'm going to whip your ass.

TRAJAN: Uh-oh, it's a low barometer day. He'll start like frothing at the mouth any second now!

DY: Danny! Please, just untie one arm! I have to smack him one.

DANNY: Yo! Show some respect! He's your brother, brothers should love one another.

PUER: [*Very interested*] Oh really? Have you a brother, Danny?

DANNY: Two of them, older.

PUER: And were you close as kinder—I mean, children?

DANNY: Sure, we was always together. Now, they think I'm a spaz and Pasquale, he keeps threatening me with the Police Force so I gotta be tough with you guys.

PUER: But did you love them and they you?

DANNY: What kinda question is that? Of course!

PUER: So you see Dy, Danny has brothers and is not afraid to say he loves them.

DY: He's Italian!

TRAJAN: And a killer.

DANNY: I'm half Irish and I never hurt a flea so you watch out or I'll break your head. Now, be quiet, all of youse!

TRAJAN: [*After a moment*] Well, Dy, do you plan on including this as an episode in your autobiography? I assume you're still writing everything down?

PUER: Indeed, he is very serious about his writing. He has promised that I will compile the index.

TRAJAN: You probably won't live to, it'll have to be published posthumously. But it'll certainly make a racy read: Killed in a homosexual's den, fighting the Mafia.

DY: Oh, Trajan, you're such a dork. This isn't a homosexual's den.

PUER: Not at all. It is a homosexual's loft.

TRAJAN: Mom will be thrilled if I live to tell her. You always were a pain in the ass but none of us thought you were a fruit. And choosing a homely old man named Beatrice to do it with ... At least Uncle Teddy looks distinguished.

DANNY: Uncle Teddy?

TRAJAN: The family skeleton!

DY: Well, Trajan you haven't changed: Perception on Parade! I'm not a fruit, as you put it, I'm not doing anything with Beatrice who is ten times the man Uncle Teddy is, and about a thousand times more alive and interesting! Look, Danny and Puer, look at my brother, the living symbol of the poverty of the upper class American life!

TRAJAN: Oh yeah! At least I'm not chasing after some weirded-out older queen in Soho!

DANNY: You're real low consciousness, you know that? If you wasn't tied up, I'd smack you myself!

TRAJAN: Low consciousness? How am I low consciousness?

DANNY: Usin' words like old and queen and homely! It ain't age or havin' balls or not havin' them, or bein' attractive that makes a person worthwhile. It's the person, it's affection. Sure, a woman's great. I'm about to get married to a woman with great potential. But not everybody wants a woman, or can find one. And even if a person wants a woman and finds one eventually doesn't mean he can find her just when he needs some affection from a nice person, you understand? [*The boys, uncomfortable in their bonds, have not followed his argument.*] Tell you what, why don't I fix up this water pipe? [*He has found the bhang* DY *purchased in Act Two.*] I got some good sensimilla in my pocket. We'll smoke a little, that'll pass the time.

DY: Can't we be untied?

DANNY: It's not that I don't trust you, I don't trust you.

PUER: Oh, but you can trust *me,* Danny.

DANNY: I can?

PUER: [*With great sincerity*] Absolutely.

DANNY: Swear by something.

PUER: My mother.

DANNY: She's a terrorist for Christ's sake!

PUER: My future.

DANNY: What if the world goes to pieces? There won't be a future. Nah, nah, I better not.

PUER: Can't I at least watch you prepare the pipe? I would like to learn.

DANNY: Yo, learn? You don't learn. You just do it one day!

PUER: Ah, as in ejaculation.

TRAJAN: Whoa, you are really strange. What's your name again?

PUER: [*Haughty*] Puer for boy. [TRAJAN *laughs*]

DY: It's no worse than Trajan and it makes a hell of a lot more sense. Come on, Danny, please let him watch.

DANNY: Tell you what, I'll untie your feet so you can walk.
PUER: [*As* DANNY *unties his feet*] Thank you, Danny.
DANNY: [*To* PUER] Come on [*He and* PUER *head for the kitchen*]
I need a strainer and some water ... [*He picks up the bhang then frowns over at* DY *and* TRAJAN.] Yo! No funny business!
[DANNY *and* PUER *go into the kitchen,* DY *and* TRAJAN *wait a minute then struggle vigorously with their bonds.*]
DY: [*To* TRAJAN] Come on, hop over to me, let's work at the ropes.
TRAJAN: Why do I have to hop to you? I'm older! You hop to me!
DY: You were the superstar gymnast, you hop over here.
TRAJAN: No!
DY: Oh fuck you!
TRAJAN: Fuck you too! [*A pause, they both work at their ropes, sulking—*TRAJAN *decides to be the mature one.*] Okay, I'll hop to you. [*He hops over to* DY, *they stand back to back and tug at the knots, ineffectually.*] This isn't going to work!
DY: [*Still working*] It always does on TV. Come on, I need to get to that restaurant and rescue Beatrice.
TRAJAN: He's the first person you ever loved isn't he?
DY: You know, Trajan, that's your problem; everything is sex to you!
TRAJAN: No, I mean in the more universal sense, like a father or brother...
DY: Oh well, maybe. [*Works at the ropes with renewed vigor*] Come on, you always had long fingers...
TRAJAN: I'm kind of sorry about that...
DY: It's too late to start apologizing for your deformities!
TRAJAN: I'm not talking about my fingers, jerk-off—I'm talking about the way you feel about this guy Beatrice... [DANNY *suddenly appears in the kitchen doorway*]
DANNY: Yo! Separate youse two or I'll hogtie you! [TRAJAN *hops across the room*] I gotta go back in—Beatrice's strainer is all clogged with old spaghetti. I schive [*A South Philly slang word for loathe*] old spaghetti, especially those thick twisted ones. They look like somebody dumped cut up arms and legs down the garbage disposal...
PUER: [*Calling from the kitchen*] Danny! Where are you?
DANNY: Coming, Puer! [*To* DY *and* TRAJAN] Stay put! [*Goes into*

the kitchen. DY *and* TRAJAN *struggle some more.*]

TRAJAN: Our working together to loosen the ropes like didn't work.

DY: I didn't think it would! Fat chance our like cooperating on anything!

TRAJAN: You know, I don't like your attitude. Any other kid brother'd be pleased his older brother had come looking for him!

DY: Oh, pardon me while I barf! Dad must have bought your way into Harvard!

TRAJAN: Yeah, big man? Well, if we live, let's just compare board scores in a year or two. And from the way the rector at St. Paul's rolled his eyes about you when I spoke to him last week, I'd like to see what kind of recommendations you get!

DY: You mean you were talking to him about me? Spying?!

TRAJAN: No, dad asked me to go back and talk to everybody who knew you there to like see if they had any ideas about where you might have gone. The rector said if you came back you could do like an independent study—since you've been in New York you could do it in Urban Squalor.

DY: Yeah, me go back to St. Paul's...!

TRAJAN: But I spent my break looking for you.

DY: I didn't ask you to! Why'd you do it anyway?

TRAJAN: Well, mom and dad are going crazy. All they do is sit around and cry. And like the worst part of it is they feel like guilty—dad especially. He's really aged and all. I mean they've hired a detective and bugged all the police stations and spent all this money but they feel—well—inadequate. You know how hard that is for dad.

DY: So super-hero Trajan has to solve it all!

TRAJAN: Well, like I did find you, you have to hand me that. It was pure and simple sugar craving that pulled me into that Mickey D's—talk about luck!

DY: [*Calling off*] Danny! What's taking so long!

TRAJAN: Why are you calling him?

DY: Because I can't stand you! Anything is better, even him!

TRAJAN: God, I'm sorry! I guess I am kind of a dork—I'm trying to work it out with my shrink at school—don't tell mom and dad. Besides, and look, don't get carried away but I felt guilty too. I felt I owed you something after pushing you out of that window. And like you have to go back... [DANNY *and* PUER *enter with water pipe and a tray of Haagen-Dazs and Sarah Lee.*]

DANNY: I brought munchies for after we're stoned.

TRAJAN: How're we gonna eat them?

DANNY: I'll figure a way. [*He smokes*] Here. [*He holds the pipe for* TRAJAN. TRAJAN *has an idea.*]

TRAJAN: [*For* DY*'s benefit*] Oh, maybe I better not.

DANNY: Come on, don't be a party pooper!

TRAJAN: But Dy, like you know what pot does to me...

DY: No I... [*Realizes something is afoot*] Oh yes—maybe you shouldn't Trajan...

TRAJAN: No, I guess I'll risk it! [*Takes a shallow puff*]

DANNY: [*To* PUER] Your turn...

PUER: How wonderful to have this experience at last! [*Smokes*]

DY: How are you feeling Trajan...?

TRAJAN: [*Getting closer to* DANNY] Weird...

DANNY: This is good stuff. [*Smokes*] Maybe smoking it'll make you wiser. [*Offers some to* DY *who takes a shallow puff, then to* TRAJAN.]

TRAJAN: What do you mean? [*Smokes*]

DANNY: I didn't like your attitude back there running down Beatrice and rushin-in to judge your brother. What would be the difference if they was having sex, hanh? [PUER, *getting giddy, smokes*] I'm not saying they are but so what if they was? [*Smokes,* DY *and* TRAJAN *make eye contact*] I don't mean no disrespect but this is my observation: it's nice in life when two people get together and hold one another, no matter what their sex is. [PUER *smokes then exhales, stoned*]

PUER: Oh, I am so glad that warmth can be found in reality and is not just a cruel illusion nurtured by the emotionally deprived ... [*Starts to giggle uncontrollably*] Oh, mein Gott, mein Gott...

DY: I think he's wasted.

PUER: This is my first time with controlled substances! [PUER *laughs wildly.* TRAJAN *catches* DY*'s eye;* DY *nods imperceptively while* DANNY, *delighted by* PUER *takes a deep pull on the pipe.*]

TRAJAN: [*Acting cramped*] Oh, I have to go to the bathroom.

DANNY: Hold it.

TRAJAN: [*Groaning up a storm*] I can't! You see, that's what I meant. Dope does this to me ... [*Groans*]

DY: Yeah, that pot gives him like diarrhea!

PUER: Diarrhea? That means ... [*Realizes what it means, howls with laughter*]

DANNY: [*Stoned, worried*] Look, I don't want no vile smells; that's one thing I schive—vile smells!

TRAJAN: Oh please, like untie me or I'll let loose right here!

DANNY: I'll untie your feet ... [*Does so.* TRAJAN *decisively kicks him in the groin;* DY *who has crowded up behind* DANNY *also pushes into him.* DANNY *befuddled by dope falls over.* PUER *runs and sits on him, giggling.*]

DY: Good Trajan—that was a great idea. Now, come on! [*They hop together and try to untie each other. They can't.*] Come on over here, Puer, and gnaw the ropes! [PUER *thinks this is hilarious*] I'm serious.

PUER: [*Suddenly solemn*] You are right. My mother, Henrietta the Terrorist told me always to try and gnaw the ropes were I bound by strangers the last time I saw her on visitation day at the prison ... [*Thinks for a moment, then whoops with laughter.*]

DY: You see what dope does?

TRAJAN: I'll gnaw the ropes. [*Kneels to do so.*]

DY: Quick, I hear somebody coming... [PATRICIA *opens the door of the loft.* PASQUALE *pushes the handcuffed* BEATRICE *in front of him.* PASQUALE *sees* DANNY *rolling on the floor and pulls his gun.*]

PASQUALE: Yo! What is all this, hanh? [*Points his gun at the boys.*] Sit down all of you! [*They do. He turns to* DANNY.] As for you, fuck up, it's the Police Force!

DANNY: [*Trying to pull himself together*] Aw, boss!

PATRICIA: [*Ironically, surveying the scene*] Just think, Beatrice, it's little boys bound! This disproves all the bad reviews which said your fiction wasn't like life!

PUER: [*Defiantly*] Just remember: The force of good prevails in his fiction, you villainess!

BEATRICE: Let them go, Patricia.

PASQUALE: [*Enjoying* BEATRICE'*s fear*] Oh no. No way. You have to learn a lesson. My papa, Cumbar' Antonio said so, and I ain't forgettin' those tactless remarks you made about my complexion!

BEATRICE: But I said I'd go back to Patricia! What more do youwant?

DY: You didn't, Beatrice!

PUER: No!

PASQUALE: Shut up, you two! I'd order you gagged but I want Beatrice to hear the screams!

PATRICIA: [*Bothered by his tone*] Now, look, Pasquale...

BEATRICE: Leave the kids out of this, Pasquale. They're harmless. If you want to hurt me, okay but...

PASQUALE: [*Gleeful*] You can't do anything about it, can you? Big writer, big artist, big word slinger—and you're helpless! Ain't that the way it always is? And the big joke of it is I envied you back then, Beatrice—you were so funny, seemed so talented. And me with my acne and body odor—I admit it, I ain't got nothin' to hide—I *smelled*—it seemed like I was the loser. But all along I suspected you was, Beatrice, and I was right! Bart Dante—the pansy flop!

DY: Beatrice! Did you really say you'd go back to her—why?

BEATRICE: Oh come on, Dy, you know why. Just be quiet now and...

DY: No! I won't be quiet! [*To* PASQUALE] Come on, torture me if you have to, but leave Beatrice alone!

TRAJAN: [*In mortal terror*] Excuse me, sir, please ignore my brother. It's a low barometer day and he becomes manic depressive...

DY: Shut up, Trajan! [*To* PASQUALE] I mean it.

PUER: [*To* PASQUALE] No! Torture me! He is his son. I am disposable!

PATRICIA: [*Sarcastic*] They think they're in an opera!

PUER: I think I am in an opera, he thinks he is in *Soldier of Fortune.*

BEATRICE: Please, Patricia, let them go!

DANNY: Yeah!

PASQUALE: [*Pushing* DANNY *aside*] Shut up, Patrolman Danny, or you won't live to take the bribes!

TRAJAN: I don't know about the German boy, miss, but my brother is overwrought. He's my kid brother and goes on and on but my folks have a lot of money and I'm sure there'd be a nice ransom if we lived.

DY: [*About* TRAJAN] He is nothing. Let him go. But if you need to hurt me, I'm here. And Beatrice, let them do it to me if that's what they want. I believe in you.

PUER: He is right. If we must suffer so you will create then so be it!

PASQUALE: Danny—gag them!

PATRICIA: No, let them talk. You two take him seriously as a writer. But have you read any of his writing by chance? Perhaps he won't be able to write anymore if he comes back to me, but that's hardly a great loss for Western Civilization. He's lost whatever talent he had, whatever seriousness.

PUER: Maybe so, but who are we to judge? Talent and seriousness—don't they start with belief? If he can no longer believe in himself then we must lend him our belief. Maybe he isn't worth it; who can say? But you are Catholics are you not? You believe in miracles don't you? So perhaps our suffering will work the miracle and the fire of art will descend on him like the Holy Gost.

PASQUALE: This is the queerist kid I've ever seen.

PUER: You are laughing. This Mafia confuses me. You romanticize yourselves as criminals yet all I see around me here is a more virulent strain of the middle class. So please laugh at me—the hopes of others are always funny to those who have never learned to hope or feel or need or dream. Come prepare to torture me, I am ready!

DY: [*Moved*] Puer, *you* are my brother.

PUER: [*Very seriously to* DY] Your brother? I have found my brother. I am ready then. Let us choose, my brother, to believe in angels and assume they will know of our agony and perhaps lend some other suffering creature our courage.

DY: Wow! Like angels!

TRAJAN: I'm going to be sick!

DY: Let's sing as they torture us!

PUER: Yes, my brother, let us sing! [DY *starts to sing "We Shall Overcome." *PUER *joins in.* DANNY, *weeping, kneels with the boys and sings along.* PASQUALE *produces his gun and puts it against* PUER'*s head. All singing stops.*]

PASQUALE: I hate music. [*Makes a move to hurt* PUER]

PATRICIA: Stop, Pasquale.

PASQUALE: What?

PATRICIA: I'm not going to let you hurt the kids, or Beatrice or anybody. Get out!

PASQUALE: But Papa said...

PATRICIA: I'm overruling Papa.

PASQUALE: Now, wait, Patty...

PATRICIA: Shut up.

PASQUALE: And this jerk? [*Roughly pushes* BEATRICE *towards her*] You still want him back?

PATRICIA: No. Take off his handcuffs.

PASQUALE: But ... I have to call Papa...

PATRICIA: Give me the fuckin' key! [*Grabs the key from the bewildered* PASQUALE] Untie the kids, Danny.

DANNY: [*Glad to obey*] Yo!

TRAJAN: [*As* DANNY *unties him*] This sure beats a weekend at Wellesley.

PASQUALE: [*To* TRAJAN *while* DY *is being untied*] And you! Don't go shooting your mouth off about this or it's your kneecaps!

TRAJAN: I won't sir, I promise!

PASQUALE: And as for your brother ... [*Turns to* DY]

PATRICIA: [*Impatient*] Just get out of here, Pasquale. Go tell Papa what I did, I'll face him later.

DANNY: [*Who has untied* PUER] Oh, boss?

PASQUALE: [*Mean*] Oh, Patrolman?

DANNY: You ain't my boss no more. I'm quitting you and I ain't joinin' no Police Force. If two kids can stand up to you, I sure as hell can. And if my mother and brothers don't like that, then fuck'em!

PUER: Bravo, Danny.

DANNY: I got my fiance. She's been after me to do this all along.

PASQUALE: We'll see about all this you dumb shit!

DANNY: Oh yeah? Well, see about this! [*Socks* PASQUALE, *knocks him out*]

PATRICIA: Oh Danny! [*Bending over* PASQUALE] Is he okay? [*Yelling in his face*] Pasquale! Yo, Pasquale! [*To* DANNY, *annoyed*] If he needs mouth-to-mouth, *you're* giving it to him! [*Yelling some more and slapping* PASQUALE's *face*] Yo, Pasquale! Are you okay?

PASQUALE: [*Coming around*] Mama, is that you?

PATRICIA: Yeah, he's okay! [*As* PASQUALE *groans*] Look, get him out of here, then take your fiance and disappear for a while—

there's my purse, take a few hundred...

DANNY: [*Starting to help* PASQUALE *up*] No, I'm not takin' any money!

PASQUALE: [*On his feet, dazed*] Is that the ice cream truck? I wanna Mister Softee!

DANNY: [*To the boys*] Help me with him...

TRAJAN: Sure... [*Helps with* PASQUALE. *They get him outside*]

DY: [*To* BEATRICE *who has been standing by, morose, silent*] Beatrice—Beatrice?

PATRICIA: Let him alone for now—you and Puer go have lunch or play video games or pick up some whores... [*Throws some money to* PUER]

DY: I think I should stay...

PUER: No, my brother, let them talk...

DY: We'll be hanging around outside, Beatrice. [*They leave.* BEATRICE *and* PATRICIA *are alone*]

PATRICIA: Well...

BEATRICE: [*Suddenly manic, avoiding her*] Oh, here's a tray of runny Haagen-Dazs and room temperature Sarah Lee. [*He has found Danny's "munchies"*] That's how you're supposed to serve them, but I never have the patience to wait. Want some?

PATRICIA: No thanks.

BEATRICE: Those pig's feet at La Gioconda are disturbing.

PATRICIA: I was moved by those boys, especially by your son. They believe in you.

BEATRICE: [*Eating, sincere*] That's strange, isn't it?

PATRICIA: Maybe, but I understand them.

BEATRICE: I wish I did.

PATRICIA: They see what I saw all those years ago when we used to sit around and read and talk about life. I thought you were the greatest. I didn't need to overlook your craziness because I thought that was part of it. That's what I told Papa when he said I was being a patsy wanting to marry you. "He'll grow up," I said, "He'll realize his potential. And Papa, it'll all be through me." Wasn't there a pop song about "girlish pride" in our youth? Well, that was me. You're a sprite, Beatrice, and sprites don't grow up, they just wither. But God knows you sure can be seductive.

BEATRICE: [*Mouth full of Sarah Lee*] Sure you don't want some?

PATRICIA: And all this melodrama today—it's because I miss you. I was willing to do anything to get you back, even alienate you. You talk a lot about being lonely, and I guess you are. But you know, I don't think you mind. I mind. You were my best friend, my son, and my teddy bear. It was all part of it that you weren't big on the pelvic action. Hell, what's so great about fucking, hanh? Yeah, maybe I will have some of the cake—I was too upset to eat the cannolis at La Gioconda. [*He gives her a slice*] Too sweet. Well, I guess I'm one neurotic broad, hanh? So, now you can have the kids, in any sense you want. I wonder if you'll disappoint them? You're like Peter Pan to them, an ancient kid. But they'll grow up and see you clearly all of a sudden. And then I wonder if they'll hate the waste of faith and cringe at all that high flown sentiment.

BEATRICE: Peter Pan, huh? No, this is Soho. It would have to be Peter Panic. Peter Panic and Trendy.

PATRICIA: Can't be serious, can you?

BEATRICE: What do you want from me? I'm a washout, a failure, I accept that. I disappointed you, forgive me. But that doesn't make you an innocent victim of my machinations. You embarked on some mystery trip with me. Who knows why? Maybe we were both neurotic outcasts unlucky enough to have too much in common for a time. But mystery trips end, period. And no one is to blame.

PATRICIA: Are you and what's his name, Dy, going to be lovers?

BEATRICE: I thought your long speech was an indirect apology for your manipulativeness? Why don't you just get out?!

PATRICIA: Oh, I know, there's nothing sexual. But what happens the night you're horny and lonely and in love? He's not much older than your son.

BEATRICE: He's old enough to consent.

PATRICIA: Oh yes, consent. Sure he is. And this disease?

BEATRICE: First of all, I don't think sex is an issue. Secondly, even if it is, I had the test as well you know during the first panic. Do you think I don't know that if you thought I was a carrier you would have moved to Mars to avoid me?

BEATRICE: So you have thought about sex with him?

BEATRICE: Of course I have, I'm not denying that...

PATRICIA: I thought one of the drives of the artist was to be a moralist?

PATRICIA

BEATRICE: Are you having an allergic reaction to the Sarah Lee, or is it to the violence you and your lovely family engineered? ~~BEATRICE:~~ If you seduce this boy where's the morality? Have you thought of the consequences for him? He loves you I think. But not the way one gay man loves another. And this won't be some anonymous trick in a men's room or some kid acting out his curiosity. This is love. And don't you wonder about his parents? I know you don't care for your son, but I bet they adore this kid and are worried silly. Do you think he should just forget about them, about his education and stay at McDonald's? And suppose you and he do become lovers— what happens when he turns twenty and is no longer attractive to you?

BEATRICE: Where is my Bartlett's quotations? Where? [*Rummages in his bookcase and finds a beat up Bartlett's*] Now let me see ... [*Consults the index then reads sarcastically, faintly campy*] "The folly of mistaking a paradox for a discovery, a metaphor for a proof, a torrent of verbiage for a spring of capital truths, and oneself for an oracle is inborn in us."[*Slams the book shut*]

PATRICIA: [*Ironic*] Isn't that a Paul Valery quote? [*She gets her purse and prepares to leave*] Well, you keep up that second hand dipping into better writers, Beatrice, in between debauches. [*Walks out*]

BEATRICE: [*Calling out after her*] Debauches, yo, fuck you, debauches! [*he puts the Bartlett's back, and clearly more upset than he let on to* PATRICIA, *clears the Sarah Lee and Haagen-Dazs, taking them into the kitchen.* DY, *much concerned, peeks in, then enters. He is alone.*]

DY: Beatrice? [BEATRICE *comes out of the kitchen*]

BEATRICE: Hi.

DY: Like hi. Trajan went off with Danny. Puer went somewhere too. I saw her leave. Was she vicious?

BEATRICE: Well, she mixed in some truth with her viciousness— that's called the unkindest cunt of all. Oops, I can't talk like that with you here.

DY: Sure you can. [*He tries to relax, so does* BEATRICE *who starts trying to straighten up the loft.* DY *gets his notebook*] This has been some adventure, you know? I can't wait to start writing it down. [*He settles down to write in his book, but realizes*

BEATRICE *is upset. He looks up after a minute, concerned.*]
Like—can I ask? What's wrong?
BEATRICE: Maybe it's the rum cannolis. I had six.
DY: [*Laughing*] Six?!
BEATRICE: Well, for one thing, pig's feet give me a craving for sweets. For another thing I thought they were the last things I'd eat on this earth and I wanted to enter paradise with that taste in my mouth.
DY: Like, what are pig's feet?
BEATRICE: Have you ever thought about having sex with me?
DY: Like no. Should I have?
BEATRICE: Pig's feet are ... well, pickled pig's feet ... washed and sauteed for hours in tomato sauce. What if we were to?
DY: What if we were to what?
BEATRICE: What if we were to ... well, you know.
DY: I thought we were friends.
BEATRICE: Well, friends have sex sometimes.
DY: I see. I guess they do. Pickled pig's feet? What does that mean?
BEATRICE: Well, it's a way of treating the feet once they cut them off—I'm getting nauseous!
DY: [*After a moment, referring to sex between them*] Why? I mean, like why all of a sudden?
BEATRICE: I've wanted to since the first night, when you appeared at the door, drenched and sick. I've watched you get dressed and undressed. I've sneaked in here some nights just to watch you sleep. I thought just being around you might be enough. I was lying to myself. I love you.
DY: Oh, I love you too. I've never had sexual feelings about you, though. But you know, like I haven't had that many sexual feelings at all—not in any concrete way. Being around you has been great. Well, maybe ... sure, if you want to.
BEATRICE: Are you sure?
DY: I love you. I want to stay with you. If that's the price I have to pay... [DY *goes into* BEATRICE*'s arms. A long embrace.*]
DY: I think like maybe we should lock the door in case the others come back. [DY *locks the door. He approaches* BEATRICE *who caresses him.* BEATRICE *kisses* DY. *This embarrasses* DY *and reflexively he pulls back. He catches himself and smiles at* BEATRICE, *then hugs him.* BEATRICE *takes* DY *by the hand and*

they go to the rollaway bed. BEATRICE *gently removes* DY's
*shirt. He takes a long time putting the shirt down, then
squarely faces* DY. *He realizes the chest is hairless, undeveloped,
softly he touches* DY.]
BEATRICE: [*Smiles*] You are a boy, aren't you? Not a fantasy but
a real boy, three dimensions of feeling with a future ... a real
boy. You know I dreamed of this moment. and maybe three
weeks ago it wouldn't have been such a bad thing. At worst it
would have been a meaningless gesture, only one in a life made
up of thousands of meaningless gestures, and both of us would
simply have forgotten it. But now—now there's too much
involved.
DY: We can do it if you want...
BEATRICE: But what about what you want? Sure I'd enjoy getting
off with you but maybe I'm old enough to live without it. And
maybe you wouldn't enjoy it...
DY: I don't know if I would or not...
BEATRICE: Well ... [*Once again caresses* DY, *very slowly, as
though trying to memorize all the contours of his body, the feel
of his skin, the potential of this moment*] I can't ... I love you
but love doesn't always have to include sex ... get dressed. [DY
puts on his shirt] You know, I wonder about your staying here.
I couldn't tonight but some other time...
DY: I understand. You're right, I guess. God, I don't want to go
back. You saw my brother, that's what they're like.
BEATRICE: You have to grow up. Somewhere inside here I'm still
your age and want all the options people your age have. I want
to be everything, a universe of possibility constantly expanding.
But I'm just me; and this tiny dust cloud is shrinking every
second. Go back and be the age you are—make your peace
with your people, painful as that is—
DY: You know, I feel like it means dying a little too ... And you
too, you must get on with your life, write and all and I'd just be
a burden...
BEATRICE: No.
DY: No. [*He smiles and touches* BEATRICE] Let's pretend then.
It'll make it easier. Well, we finally have a use for your phone.
I'll call them collect.
BEATRICE: Oh no, dial direct, I owe them a lot.
DY: [*Dials*] Hello, mom? Like this is Dy. Yes, Dy. I'm fine ... I'm

coming home. Tonight. Sure, is he there? [*Waits, he looks at* BEATRICE *who is staring at him*] Dad? Hi, dad, I'm fine, no, I'm fine. Dad? [*To* BEATRICE, *very surprised*] He's crying. [TRAJAN *knocks at the door.* BEATRICE *unlocks it and lets him in.* TRAJAN *has had his hair styled in the most new wave fashion and also bought some decidedly strange looking new wave clothes. He struts in showing them off, carrying his old clothes in a bag.* DY *sees him and bursts out laughing.*] Oh, dad, wait until you see Trajan!

TRAJAN: [*To* DY] You mean you called dad? [*To* BEATRICE] He called my parents? [BEATRICE *nods yes, then walks out of the room*]

DY: See you later, dad—yeah, I'm fine! Bye. [*He hangs up*]

TRAJAN: [*To* DY, *annoyed*] You're so fucking perverse! I spent all this money getting ready for a night on the town!

DY: I'll go alone!

TRAJAN: Oh that's right, rob me of my victory in finding you ... [*Realizes he's being childish*] I'm sorry. Are you okay? [*Nodding to where* BEATRICE *has gone off*] Is he okay? I mean, I can leave you two alone for awhile...

DY: No, you don't need to ... [*Sets about gathering his few possessions*]

TRAJAN: The car's in that lot near McDonald's...

DY: Shit, now I won't be able to give notice.

TRAJAN: Write them. I'll go bring the car around front. [*Calls off*] Goodbye Mister Dante, it's been unusual. I'll be outside, Dy. [*Leaves.* BEATRICE *appears, determined not to make a scene.*]

DY: Well ... goodbye.

BEATRICE: Goodbye. [*They shake hands*]

DY: Would you like my book? [*Holds out the notebook*]

BEATRICE: *Coming of Age in Soho?* Oh, no...

DY: Keep it. Just send me a xerox of it—my address is in there...

BEATRICE: [*Touched*] Thanks.

DY: I'm going to run now because if I stay I'll start to cry and I'm too old to cry ... [*Runs out*]

BEATRICE: [*Alone*] I'm not ... [*Cries silently. He folds up the rollaway bed.* PUER *enters. He is dressed as he was when we first saw him. He has depunked himself. He comes in wheeling* Death in Venice, BEATRICE's *game, in front of him.*]

PUER: I returned to Patricia's and retrieved what I left there. With the money she threw me I rescued *Death in Venice* from the pawn shop. Goodbye father.

BEATRICE: You're going?

PUER: Yes. I don't belong here. I am hitchhiking to the airport where I will stow away back to Germany.

BEATRICE: Goodbye then.

PUER: I don't know what I shall do there. I suspect they will refuse to take me back in the school. Perhaps I shall simply die. [BEATRICE *starts to weep loudly, uncontrollably.* PUER *stands watching him, uncertain what to do.*] I'm sorry, I was being self-dramatic, I won't die ... [BEATRICE *collapses to the floor.* PUER *waits a moment. Then he closes the door to the street. He removes his backpack and deliberately walks to* BEATRICE. *He kneels beside him and takes him into his arms, cradling him with the utmost tenderness.*] Father? I can take your suffering on myself. I am your son and I love you. I give you that love. I am not so foolish a child as to think it will matter so much. But I give it to you with all my heart. And if you accept it, perhaps we can both hope. You gave me my life, and I love my life. I love consciousness and the knowledge of being. I want to give them back to you ... let me hold you ... [*He holds him.* BEATRICE *calms himself, and finally sits up. He takes* PUER*'s face in his hands.*]

BEATRICE: I don't love you and should I pretend? I have so little to offer you ... but, all right, for the first time I will acknowledge you as my son. We are both placeless people, but I recognize you. And you know when you held me—it helped. Do you think I could market you as a little boy healer and make us both a fortune. [*Hugs* PUER] There it is again—that feeling! [*Hugs him tighter*] My son. [*Thinks about that phrase for a moment*] No, don't die, my son. I don't want to die either. I love life too. But there are practical issues here, like how are we going to live? [*Stands up*] I'll tell you what, take Dy's book and let's put it on this fucking computer. Maybe there's something in there about me, or about us, or maybe about the three of us I can expand...

PUER: [*Happy*] You are willing to work?

BEATRICE: Maybe fail...

PUER: [*Running to the computer, turning it on and getting*

ready] Simply to make the attempt is not to fail!
BEATRICE: All right—I'm going to read this book—and you type into that thing everything that rings a bell. And maybe I'll free-associate. I've got to get a diet Pepsi...
PUER: [*Busy at the console*] Please, one for me as well.
BEATRICE: [*Bearing two diet Pepsi's*] All right! [*Thinks, then declaims*] It was the worst of times but Bartholomew Dante began to come of age, and this is his story!

BLACKOUT

Gemini

Characters

FRAN GEMINIANI is forty-five, working-class, boisterous, and friendly. He is slightly overweight, coughs a lot from mild emphysema.

FRANCIS GEMINIANI, his son, is about to celebrate his twenty-first birthday. He is also plump, a little clumsy, is entering his senior year at Harvard.

LUCILLE POMPI is Fran's lady friend, very thin, early forties, working-class, but strives hard to act in accordance with her ideas of ladylike behavior and elegance.

BUNNY WEINBERGER, the Geminiani's next-door neighbor, is a heavyset, blowsy woman, about forty, once very beautiful and voluptuous, now rough-talking and inclined to drink too much.

HERSCHEL WEINBERGER, her son, is sixteen, very heavy, asthmatic, very bright, but eccentric. He is obsessed with public transportation in all its manifestations and is shy and a little backward socially.

JUDITH HASTINGS, Francis's classmate at Harvard, is a month or two younger than Francis. She is an exceedingly, perhaps even intimidatingly, beautiful Wasp. She is extremely intelligent, perhaps slightly more aggressive than she should be, but is basically well-meaning.

RANDY HASTINGS, her brother, has just finished his freshman year at Harvard. Like Judith, he is a quintessential, very handsome Wasp.

The play takes place on June 1 and 2, 1973. The latter marks Francis's twenty-first birthday.

Scenes

ACT I
Scene 1: June 1, 1973. Early morning.
Scene 2: That evening.

ACT II
Scene 1: June 2, 1973. Morning.
Scene 2: That evening.

The setting shows the backyards of two adjoining row houses in the Italian section of South Philadelphia. They are small, two-story, brick houses typical of the poorer sections of most big cities. In one house live the Geminianis, Fran and Francis, and in the other the Weinbergers, Bunny and Herschel. In the Geminiani yard is a fig tree, and along one side a high alley fence with a gate. The Weinberger yard contains an old ladder, a rusty old tricycle, garbage cans, and a certain amount of general debris, and is also bounded by an alley wall, behind which is a high utility or telephone pole.

ACT I

Scene 1

The sound of garbage men emptying the garbage in the alley. They are making an immense noise. It is just past dawn and they are banging lids, overturning cans, and yelling to one another.

FRANCIS GEMINIANI appears at his bedroom window. He is dressed in a T-shirt, his hair is wild, his glasses are awry. He has just been awakened and is in a rage.

FRANCIS: Shut up! Will you please shut up! Why aren't you men more civilized? Oh, Jesus Christ!
[*He sets a speaker on the windowsill, and turns on the final portion full blast of Isolde's narrative and curse from Act I of* Tristan und Isolde. BUNNY WEINBERGER *appears at the second-floor window of her house. She is in a torn nightgown and faded robe, and is also in a rage.*]
BUNNY: Francis! Francis! Why are you playing that music at six o' clock in the mornin'? You got somethin' against my gettin' a good night's sleep?
FRANCIS: [*Leaning out his window.*] Do you hear the garbage men?
BUNNY: Sure. They're just doing their job. That's the trouble wit you college kids—got no respect for the working man. Besides, I got an uncle out there. [*Shouts out to alley behind fence.*] Hi ya, Uncle Jerry!
VOICE: [*From behind the fence*] Hi ya, Bun!
BUNNY: How's your hammer hanging? [*Then to* FRANCIS] See, I got connections. You stick wit me, kid, I'll get you a job. [*A knocking is heard at the front door of the*

Geminiani house.] And now you got them knockin' at your door. You woke everybody up. Ain't you gonna answer it?

FRANCIS: I'm going back to bed. [*He takes the speaker off the sill.*]

BUNNY: Good. Maybe we'll have some quiet.

[*She disappears inside her bedroom. The knocking continues. The garbage men fade away.* FRANCIS *has now put on a very quiet passage from Act IV of Verdi's* I Vespri Siciliani. *After a moment, a knocking is heard at the gate in the fence, the entrance to the Geminiani yard.* FRANCIS *does not come to his window. More knocking. A pause. Then a rolled-up sleeping bag comes sailing over the fence, followed by a small knapsack.* RANDY HASTINGS *appears at the top of the fence. He climbs over and jumps into the yard. He looks around. Suddenly a large knapsack, the kind that has an aluminum frame, appears at the top of the fence.* RANDY *takes it and puts it down on the ground. Next we see a rolled-up tent, a second sleeping bag on the fence, then a tennis racket, and then* JUDITH HASTINGS. *She perches on top of the fence, looks around, and then jumps into the yard.* RANDY *has piled everything neatly together in the middle of the yard. They are both in worn jeans and sneakers. They circle about the yard, peeking into* BUNNY's *part curiously.* JUDITH *notices the fig tree and smiles. She knocks at the back door. No answer.* RANDY *tries to open it, but it is latched from the inside. He then peeks into the window to the left of the door and sees* FRANCIS *sleeping in his room. He smiles at* JUDITH, *and they climb into* FRANCIS's *room.*]

JUDITH *and* RANDY: Surprise! Surprise!

[*The music stops.* FRANCIS *leaps out of bed.*]

JUDITH: [*Inside the room*] Put your glasses on, it's Judith. . . .

RANDY: . . . and Randy. What's the matter?

FRANCIS: What are you doing here?

JUDITH: Come to see you, of course—

FRANCIS: Why?

JUDITH: It's your birthday tomorrow, your twenty-first.

[*At this moment,* HERSCHEL *dashes out of the back door of his house and into the yard. He hurls himself onto the rusty tricycle and, making subway engine noises, careens about the yard.*]

RANDY: [*Looking through screen door*] Francis, who's that?

FRANCIS: [*With* JUDITH *in kitchen window*] Herschel next door.

RANDY: What's he doing?

FRANCIS: Hey, Herschel, what are you doing?

HERSCHEL: I'm pretending I'm a subway engine.

FRANCIS: Which one?

HERSCHEL: Three nineteen AA four six five AA BZ substratum two. Built in 1945, in April, first run on Memorial Day.

FRANCIS: Herschel is into public transportation.

[BUNNY *comes out of her house, still in the same torn and smudged nightgown and housecoat. She has a quart beer bottle in one hand and a cigarette in the other.*]

BUNNY: What the fuck's goin' on out here, hanh? Why you up so early?

[HERSCHEL, *making engine noises, heads right for her. She sidesteps the tricycle easily.*]

BUNNY: Jesus Christ, it's that engine you're goin' a see.

FRANCIS: [*From window, still with* JUDITH. RANDY *has come out to get a better view.*] Bunny, these are friends of mine from school. Judith Hastings and her brother, Randy. [*Indicates* BUNNY.] This is my neighbor, Bunny Weinberger.

BUNNY: I didn't know they had girls at Harvard.

FRANCIS: Judith is at Radcliffe.

BUNNY: This is my son, Herschel. He's a genius. He's gotta IQ of 187 or 172, depending on which test you use. [*To* HERSCHEL, *who is still careening about.*] Stop that fuckin' noise! He's also got asthma, and he tends to break out.

HERSCHEL: [*To* RANDY] You want to see my collection of transfers?

RANDY: [*With a shrug*] Sure.

[HERSCHEL *dashes into his house.*]

BUNNY: [*Looking after him*] Well, all geniuses is a little crazy. You kids look hungry, so damn skinny. [*She is poking* RANDY *in the stomach.*]

RANDY: Do you think so?

BUNNY: I guess you're scholarship students at Harvard, hanh? Although Francis is on scholarship you wouldn't know it to look at him. You wan' some breakfast?

JUDITH: That would be very nice.

[BUNNY *starts for her door.*]

FRANCIS: Get the roaches out of the oven first, Bunny.

BUNNY: [*Good-naturedly*] Oh, go fuck yourself. I ain't had a live roach in here in a year, unless you count Herschel, I think he's part roach. Whatayas want? Fried eggs and bacon all right?

RANDY: Sure.

BUNNY: He's normal, at least. [*She goes inside.*]

FRANCIS: So . . . you're just here for the day?

JUDITH: For the day? Some people go away to the beach from the city, we have come away to the city from the beach.

RANDY: Can you say that in French?

JUDITH: [*Coming out of the house*] *Il y a des gens qui vont . . .*

FRANCIS: [*Interrupting*] How'd you get here?

JUDITH: We hitchhiked, of course.

FRANCIS: You rich people are crazy. It would never occur to me to hitchhike.

JUDITH: That's because you couldn't get picked up.

RANDY: Come on, Judith, you can help me set up the tent.

FRANCIS: [*From his room, putting on his pants*] Tent?

RANDY: Sure. We always sleep outside. We could put it up under this tree. What kind is it?

JUDITH: Fig, idiot.

RANDY: What's a fig tree doing in your yard?

FRANCIS: [*Coming out of house, pants on, but barefoot*] You'll have to ask my father, he planted it. But look, I don't want . . . I mean . . . well, you see, it's my father. I mean you can't stay here. He doesn't like company.

RANDY: But I thought wops loved company.

[JUDITH *hits him.*]

FRANCIS: Mafia.

JUDITH: The Mafia?

FRANCIS: You know, the Black Hand, Cosa Nostra, the Brotherhood. . . .

RANDY: Your father's in the . . .

FRANCIS: Hit man.

JUDITH: Oh, come on!

FRANCIS: He offs Wasps. It was bred into him at an early age, this raving hatred of white Anglo-Saxon Protestants, they call them white people.

RANDY: [*Looks worried.*] White people?

FRANCIS: He collects their ears after he murders them, he has a collection in his room. . . . [*Starts picking up their camping equipment and hands it to* JUDITH *and* RANDY.] I'll tell you what, let's go to the bus terminal, I'll finish getting dressed, we'll put your stuff in a locker, I'll show you around, we'll take a few pictures, then you can go back later tonight. I'll get my camera. [*He runs inside.*]

RANDY: You mean we have to carry this junk around some more?

JUDITH: [*At* FRANCIS'*s window*] Why don't you come back with us—we've got plenty of room—Mother will love you—you can cook for us.

FRANCIS: [*Appears at window.*] I can't. I have a job.

RANDY: You can watch me work out.

JUDITH: Oh, Randy, grow up! I wanted to see you . . .

FRAN: [*Offstage*] Yo, Françis, you home!

FRANCIS: Oh, Jesus Christ!

[RANDY *is trying to escape for his life.* JUDITH *is holding him back.*]

FRAN: [*Offstage, yelling*] Yo, Francis, we're back!

[FRAN *unlocks the gate, which had a chain and padlock. He appears with an empty trashcan,* LUCILLE *right behind him, holding three freshly pressed shirts on hangers.* FRAN *sets the trashcan under his kitchen window, and then notices the visitors in his yard.*]

FRAN: [*Yelling into window*] You got company?

JUDITH: [*Hastily*] My name is Judith Hastings, and this is my brother Randy. We know Francis from Harvard.

FRAN: Oh yeah? I'm his dad. I didn't know Igor had friends. He just sits around all day, no job, nothin'. My name's Francis too. [*Turns to* RANDY.] But you can call me Franny, or Fran, or Frank. [*Turns to* JUDITH.] And you can call me honey, or sweetness and light, or darling, whatever you like. [*Indicates* LUCILLE, *who is trying to blend into the fence, because she has been surprised in a housecoat.*] This is Lucille.

LUCILLE: Oh dear.

JUDITH: Well, we were just leaving.

FRAN: Leavin'? But you just got here, you can't leave.

LUCILLE: [*Attempting elegance*] Well, Fran, thanks for comin' over. . . . [*She hands* FRAN *his shirts.*] Of course, I was rather surprised, its bein' so early, my dress.

BUNNY: [*Appears in her window.*] Hi ya, Fran.

FRAN: Yo, Bun.

BUNNY: [*Sees* LUCILLE.] I see you got the Holy Clam wit you. I'm cookin' breakfast.

LUCILLE: [*To* JUDITH *and* RANDY, *still explaining*] And then I have to wash my hair. . . .

BUNNY: Shut up, Lucille, you keep washin' it and it's gonna fall out, and not just your hair. Hey, you kids, you wan' some oregano in these eggs?

FRAN: Why? They're still gonna be Irish eggs.

BUNNY: I gotta Jew name, but I'm Irish. Real name's Murphy.

FRAN: You still got roaches in that oven? [*Coughs from emphysema, then laughs.*]

BUNNY: You still got rats up your ass?

LUCILLE: Bunny! [*Then to* FRAN] Stop smoking, hanh?

BUNNY: [*In her window, with a mixing bowl, singing*]
    Oh, I got plenty of nothin'
    and nothing's got plenty of me,
    Got my ass,
    Got my tits,
    Got my cup of tea,
    Ain't no use complainin',
    Got my ass,
    Got my ass,
    Got my tits!"

[*Dialogue continues over* BUNNY's *song.*]

FRAN: [*To* RANDY *and* JUDITH] You just get here?

JUDITH: You're sure you want us to stay?

FRAN: Whataya mean am I sure?

RANDY: We're Wasps. . . .

FRAN: So? I'm broad-minded. Is that a tent?

RANDY: We like to sleep outside.

FRAN: You kids is all nuts, you know that? So put it up! [*Scratches.*]

LUCILLE: [*Setting up a lawn chair*] Stop scratching that rash.

FRAN: That's my fig tree, you know! I planted it.

[BUNNY *finishes her song and goes back to cooking.*

LUCILLE *sits down and talks to* RANDY.]

LUCILLE: So how do you do? My name is Lucille Pompi. I have a son at Yale and my daughter is a dental technician, she works at the Graduate Hospital, special shift, and my late husband ...

FRAN: *Sta'zit'*, Lucille, these kids look hungry. You must be on scholarship at Harvard, though Francis is on scholarship you'd never know it to look at him. We got lots of food in, only thing that keeps him from jumpin' out the window when he's home. [*Coughs.*]

LUCILLE: Turn away from people when you cough, hanh? [RANDY *and* JUDITH *are pitching the tent under the tree.*]

FRAN: We got brebalone and pepperoni, how 'bout some while horseshit finishes up the eggs? We also got pizzel. Francis loves them but I got a whole box hid.

JUDITH: Oh, I'm sure breakfast will be more than enough.

FRAN: But you don't understand. That's gonna be a Irish breakfast—that's a half a egg, a quarter slice a bacon. ... [*Scratches.*]

LUCILLE: [*Genteel*] The Irish mean well but they don't know how to eat. [*To* FRAN, *genteel manner gone*] Don't scratch that rash!

FRAN: I'll get everything together.

JUDITH: I'll help you.

FRAN: Well, thank you, sweetheart. What's your name again?

JUDITH: Judith.

[*He lets her go in first and admires her figure. He shakes his head appreciatively and winks at* RANDY, *who winks back, laughing.* RANDY *continues pitching the tent.*]

LUCILLE: [*To* RANDY, *after* FRAN *and* JUDITH *have exited*] My son, Donny Pompi, is at Yale, he's a sophomore on the basketball team and in pre-med. He's on a Branford scholarship. Do you know him?

RANDY: I go to Harvard.

LUCILLE: But he's at Yale. Wouldn't you know him?

RANDY: No, I go to Harvard.

LUCILLE: Is there a difference?

FRAN: [*Coming out of the kitchen, yelling*] Yo, Francis! Where's your manners? Was you raised in the jungle? [FRAN *and* JUDITH *come into the yard; he is carrying*

a typing table with a tray of food on it, and she has a
cake and napkins.]

FRAN: Sometimes I wonder about him, his mother used to say when he was born he broke the mold, maybe she was right.

[LUCILLE *starts serving and repeating absentmindedly after* FRAN.]

FRAN: Now, we got here: Coffee cake . . .

LUCILLE: Coffee cake . . .

FRAN: Jelly doughnuts . . .

LUCILLE: Jelly doughnuts . . .

FRAN: Black olives, green olives, pitted black olives—they're easier to digest, chocolate-covered doughnuts—[*He holds one up.*]—they're Francis's favorites, so eat them first and save him some pimples—brebalone, pepperoni, pizzel, biscuits, a fiadone Lucille baked last week and some hot peppers. Don't be shy.

RANDY: Thanks.

FRAN: Yo, Francis! Where the hell are you?

BUNNY: [*Enters carrying a huge tray of food.*] Here's breakfast.

[*She is followed out by* HERSCHEL, *who is carrying a huge box.* BUNNY *notices that the Geminiani tray is on a typing table, so she sets her tray on a trash can that is under her kitchen window, and drags the whole thing to the center of the yard. She hands* RANDY *a plate with a fried egg on it.*]

HERSCHEL: [*To* RANDY] Here's my collection of transfers.

RANDY: Lot of them. [*Sits down in front of tent to eat.*]

HERSCHEL: [*Following* RANDY] Four thousand seven hundred and twenty-two. They start at eighteen seventy-three.

BUNNY: Biggest collection in the state outside of a museum. That's what my uncle works at the PTC told me.

HERSCHEL: [*Opening one of the albums*] These are from the old trolleys; they're my favorites, they're buried, you see.

FRAN: Yo, Francis!

FRANCIS: [*Inside, yelling*] Jesus Christ in heaven, I'm coming.

FRAN: That's my Ivy League son.

FRANCIS: [*Entering the yard*] Lot of food.

FRAN: These kids gotta eat. Looka how skinny they are. You don' gotta eat, but that's all you do.

BUNNY: [*About* HERSCHEL, *who is gulping large quantities of food*] This is another one. Looka him put that food away. Slow down!

[HERSCHEL *chokes.*]

BUNNY: Oh, oh, he's gonna have a asthma attack. I think he does it to punish me. You ever try to sleep with someone havin' a asthma attack in the next room? Drives you bananas. [*To* HERSCHEL, *still gulping*] Take human bites, for Christ' sake! Jesus, it's like a threshing machine: Varroom! Varroom!

FRAN: [*To* JUDITH] Don't be bashful, we got plenty.

JUDITH: I'm not bashful.

FRAN: Eat, then!

BUNNY: [*Lunges at* HERSCHEL *with the fly swatter.*] Slow down! The end of the world ain't for another twenty minutes.

[*He slows down.*]

BUNNY: That's right. [*She looks at his neck.*] Look at them mosquito bites. You been pickin' them? I says, you been pickin' them?

HERSCHEL: No.

BUNNY: I told you and I told you not to pick at them, they'll get infected.

FRAN: [*To* RANDY] You got a appetite, at least.

JUDITH: [*Stands up; to* FRAN] *Egli è casa dappertutto.*

FRAN: [*Not having understood*] Hanh?

FRANCIS: She's an Italian major at Radcliffe.

JUDITH: [*Very conversationally*] *Questo giardin mi piace molto. Il nostro camino non furo facile, ma siamo giovane e . . .*

[*They all look at her, puzzled.*]

LUCILLE: You see, dear, that's Harvard Italian. We don't speak that.

FRAN: What did you say?

JUDITH: [*Very embarrassed, sits down.*] Oh, nothing.

FRAN: You see, my people over there was the niggers. The farmhands, they worked the land. We're Abruzzese; so we speak a kinda nigger Italian.

LUCILLE: Oh, Fran! He means it's a dialect.

BUNNY: [*Looking* FRAN *over mock-critically*] Niggers,

hanh? Let me look, let me look. Yeah, I thought so. Suspicious complexion.

[*She grabs his crotch.* LUCILLE *scowls.*]

FRAN: [*To* BUNNY] You're not eatin' as much as usual, Bun.

BUNNY: I'm eatin' light, got stage fright. Gotta go a court today.

FRAN: Yeah, why?

LUCILLE: Oh, Bunny, please, not in front of the kids!

BUNNY: That bitch Mary O'Donnel attacked me. I was lyin' there, mindin' my own business, and she walks in, drops the groceries, screams, then throws herself on top a me.

FRAN: Where was you lyin'?

BUNNY: In bed.

FRAN: Whose bed?

BUNNY: Whataya mean: Whose bed? Don' matter whose bed. No matter where a person is, that person gotta right to be treated wit courtesy. And her fuckin' husband was no use; he just says: Oh, Mary! turns over and goes back to sleep. So's I hadda fend for myself. She threw herself on top a me, see, so I broke her fuckin' arm. Well, you woulda thought the whole world was fuckin' endin'. She sat there and screamed. I didn't know what to do. It was her house. I didn't know where nothin' was and she's a shitty housekeeper. So I shook her fuckin' husband's arm and said get the fuck up, I just broke your fuckin' wife's arm. But he shook me off, you know how these men are, afta, so's I put on my slip, and I put on my dress and got the hell out of there. I'll tell you my ears was burnin'. That witch has gotta tongue like the murders in the Rue Morgue. Then, of all the face, she's got the guts to go to the cops and say I assaulted her. Well, I was real ashamed to have to admit I did go after Mary O'Donnel. She smells like old peanuts. Ever smell her, Lucille?

[LUCILLE *shudders and turns away.*]

BUNNY: So's I gotta go to court and stand trial. But I ain't worried. I gotta uncle on the force, he's a captain. Come on, Herschel. Sam the Jew wan's a see his kid today.

[*She picks up her tray.*]

LUCILLE: [*Not moving*] I'll help clean up.

JUDITH: [*Jumping up*] So will I.

BUNNY: Good, 'cause I gotta get ready to meet my judge. I'll show youse where everything is.

HERSCHEL: [*To* RANDY] Do you want to see my collection of subway posters?

RANDY: [*After some hesitation*] Well, all right.

HERSCHEL: [*Following* RANDY *into house, with his transfers*] I have eight hundred . . .

BUNNY: [*Holding door for* LUCILLE] Right this way, the palace is open.

[FRAN *and* FRANCIS *are left alone.*]

FRAN: I didn't know your friends was comin'.

FRANCIS: I didn't either.

FRAN: They are your friends', ain't they?

FRANCIS: It isn't that simple.

FRAN: You kids is all nuts, you know that? It was that simple when I was growin' up. You hung out on the corner, see, and the guys you hung out wit was your friends, see? Never stopped to think about it.

FRANCIS: Those guys you hung out with were pretty quick to drop you when you had all the trouble with the bookies, and when Mother left. You might say they deserted you.

FRAN: Yeah, yeah, you might say that.

FRANCIS: So then, they weren't friends.

FRAN: Course they was. People desert other people, don' make no difference if they're friends or not. I mean, if they wasn't friends to begin wit, you couldn't say they deserted me, could you?

FRANCIS: I guess not.

FRAN: Francis, this Judith, she's really somethin'. I didn't know you had the eye, you know?

FRANCIS: How was your trip to Wildwood?

FRAN: Well, Lucille had a fight wit Aunt Emma. That's why we came back. It was over water bugs. I didn't see no water bugs. But Lucille said they was everywhere. Aunt Emma thought she was accusin' her of bein' dirty. So we came back.

FRANCIS: Lucille is quite a phenomenon.

FRAN: She's good people, she means well. There ain't nothin' like a woman's company, remember that, my son, there ain't nothin' like a woman. You can think there is. I thought the horses was just as good; hell, I thought the horses was better. But I was wrong. But

you gotta be careful of white women. I guess us dagos
go afta them; hell, I went afta you mother, and she was
as white as this Judith, though not near as pretty. But
you gotta be careful of them kinda women. A white
woman's like a big hole, you can never be sure what's
in there. So you be careful, even if she is a Italian major.
What do you want for your birthday tomorrow?
[*They start clearing the yard, folding the chairs, putting trashcans back in place, typing table back in the
house.*]

FRANCIS: Not to be reminded of it.

FRAN: C'mon, we gotta do somethin'. That's a big occasion: Twenty-one! I know what! You and your guests
can have a big dinner out wit Lucille and me to celebrate.

FRANCIS: Oh, I think they'll have left by then.

FRAN: They just got here!

FRANCIS: Well, you know how these kids are nowadays,
all nuts. They can't stand to be in one place more than
a few hours.

FRAN: But they just pitched their tent under the fig tree,
even. No, no, I think you're wrong. I think we're in for
a visit. And I hope so, they seem like nice kids.

FRANCIS: Well, they're a little crazy; you know, speed, it
twists the mind.

FRAN: Speed?

FRANCIS: Yeah, they're both what we call speed freaks.
That's why they're so skinny.

FRAN: You mean they ain't on scholarship?

FRANCIS: They're on speed.

FRAN: Oh, my God, them poor kids. They need some
help. I'm gonna call Doc Pollicarpo, maybe he could
help them.
[RANDY *comes out of* BUNNY's *house, carrying heavy
books.*]

RANDY: Herschel lent me his books on subways.... [*He
sets them down in front of the tent.*]

FRAN: You poor kid.

RANDY: [*Misunderstanding*] Well ...

FRAN: No wonder you're so skinny.

RANDY: I'm not that skinny.

FRAN: Some other kid started you on it? Somebody tie
you down and force it into your veins?

RANDY: What?

FRAN: Looka his eyes—that's a real strange color. I guess that proves it. You got holes in your arms too?

RANDY: What—why?

FRAN: Come here and sit down, you need rest, you need good food, have a black olive, that's good for speed.

RANDY: [*Shocked*] Speed?

FRAN: And your sister too? That beautiful young girl on speed? It's a heartbreaker. That stuff it works fast, that's why they call it speed.

[FRANCIS *nods in agreement.*]

FRAN: You can see it rot the brain.

RANDY: But I'm not on . . . [*Looks at* FRANCIS, *understanding.*]

FRANCIS: [*Shrugs.*] My father got it in his head you were on speed.

RANDY: I never touch it.

FRAN: [*Understanding*] Oh, yeah, let's make a fool of the old man. [*Yelling*] Yo, Lucille, get the hell out here. [*To* RANDY] I'm sorry, young man, my son is a little twisted. His mother used to say when he came along he—

FRANCIS: [*Has heard this many times.*] —when he came along he broke the mold.

FRAN: [*Yelling*] Lucille! I'm not gonna call you again.

LUCILLE: [*Coming out*] I'm here. And don't scratch that rash, makes it worse.

FRAN: [*Yelling*] Yo, Bun, gook luck wit the judge! [*To* LUCILLE] Come on. [*Heads toward the kitchen, turns back.*] Randy, if you're gonna smoke pot out here, do it quiet.

LUCILLE: Oh, I'm sure he's too nice a boy to—

FRAN: Lucille, get inna house!

[FRAN, *with* LUCILLE, *enters house.*]

RANDY: What's all this about speed? That's what I call a sixties mentality.

FRANCIS: Where's Judith?

RANDY: Still cleaning up, I guess. [*Pulls out a box of joints.*] Want some pot?

FRANCIS: Why'd you come? You could have given me some warning.

RANDY: We're not an atomic attack. [*He starts boxing with* FRANCIS.]

FRANCIS: You dropped in like one.

[RANDY *starts doing push-ups.*]

FRANCIS: What are you doing?

RANDY: I've been working out every day and taking tiger's milk and nutriment. . . .

FRANCIS: What about Wate-On?

RANDY: Overrated. [*Rolls over on his back.*] Hey, hold my legs.

FRANCIS: You want to play *Sunrise at Campobello?*

RANDY: Smart ass, I want to do sit-ups.

[FRANCIS *kneels and gets a hold of* RANDY's *feet.* RANDY *starts doing sit-ups.*]

FRANCIS: [*Grunts.*] One . . . three . . . You weren't this bad last spring. Even though you did drag me to the gym once—I even had to take a shower—I stumbled around without my glasses, I couldn't see anything, my arms were out like Frankenstein's—they thought I was very strange. [*He looks down at his arms.*] My arms are getting tired—and what is this supposed to do?

RANDY: [*Still lying on the ground*] I'm tired of being skinny.

FRANCIS: You aren't that skinny.

RANDY: I'm grotesque-looking. Look at my chest. [*Lifts shirt.*] I look like a newborn duck. I want pectorals, I want biceps, I want shoulders. I want people to stop sniggering when they look at me.

FRANCIS: I don't snigger when I look at you.

RANDY: [*Seriously*] You're my friend.

[FRANCIS *rises, uncomfortable.* RANDY *lights up a joint.*]

RANDY: Is there a pool around here? I'd like to go swimming.

FRANCIS: That's a good way to get spinal meningitis. Look, Randy, don't you think I'm an unlikely choice for a jock buddy?

[JUDITH *comes out of the house and joins them on the stoop.*]

JUDITH: Sorry that took so long, but Lucille didn't do anything, she just stood there and insisted I had to know her son. Hey, Francis, how are you going to entertain me? Is there a museum in walking distance of Philadelphia?

RANDY: That's low-priority; we're going to the boat races.

JUDITH: Randy, why don't you simply realize you're pathetic, and stop boring intelligent people?

RANDY: And why don't you treat your hemorrhoids and stop acting like somebody out of Picasso's blue period. . . .

[BUNNY *comes out of her house. She is wearing a very tight white crocheted suit and carrying a plastic flowered shopping bag. She is dressed for court.*]

BUNNY: [*Strikes a "stunning" pose.*] How do I look?

RANDY: Like you can win the case.

BUNNY: You're sweet. Give me a kiss for luck. [*Grabs and kisses him. Then yells.*] Herschel! [*Back to* RANDY] Look at his skin, look at his eyes; ain't anybody around here looks like you, honey. Like a fuckin' white sheik!

[HERSCHEL *enters from his house. He is dressed for a visit with his father, in an enormous, ill-fitting brown suit.*]

BUNNY: Oh, Herschel. Come on. [*Brushes his suit roughly.*] And look you, don't you go havin' no asthma attacks wit your father, he blames me.

JUDITH: [*Suddenly*] Herschel, Randy'll go with you; he wants to go to the park and study your subway books. [*She grabs one of the big books and drops it in* RANDY's *hands.* RANDY *looks shocked.*]

HERSCHEL: [*Astounded and delighted*] Really?

JUDITH: [*Before* RANDY *can speak*] And do you happen to have, by any chance, a map of the subway system? Randy was just saying how much he wanted to study one.

HERSCHEL: Yes! [*Digs in his pockets.*] I have three. This one is the most up-to-date. You're interested—really interested?

RANDY: Well—I . . .

HERSCHEL: [*Grabbing* RANDY's *arm*] Come on, I'll walk you to the park! [*Drags* RANDY *off down the alley.*] I know the way and everything. . . .

BUNNY: [*Yelling after them*] Don't fall down, Herschel, that suit costs a fortune to clean. [*To* JUDITH *and* FRANCIS] Well, I'm off. Wish me luck.

JUDITH and FRANCIS: [*Smoking a joint*] Good luck.

BUNNY: [*Crosses to the gate.*] I'll see youse later. I mean I hope I see youse later.

[*She exits, crossing her fingers for luck.* JUDITH *passes the joint to* FRANCIS. *She goes as if to kiss him, but instead blows smoke in his mouth. He chokes.*]

FRANCIS: Did you come here to humiliate me?

JUDITH: What?

FRANCIS: What do you call coming here with your brother, climbing over the back fence, walking in on me, half-naked, unannounced? And then, Bunny, Herschel—the house is a mess—

JUDITH: That doesn't bother me, really. You oughtn't to be ashamed.

FRANCIS: Oh, I wish you hadn't come, that's all, I wish you hadn't come, you or Randy. . . .

JUDITH: But why? I took you seriously, I took—everything seriously and then I hadn't heard—

FRANCIS: I didn't want any more of either of you.

JUDITH: Francis!

FRANCIS: Have you looked at me? I'm fat!

JUDITH: You're not fat!

FRANCIS: Then what do you call this? [*Makes two rolls of fat with his hands.*] If I try I can make three—

JUDITH: You're crazy! What does that have to do with anything?

FRANCIS: No attractive person has ever been interested in me. . . .

JUDITH: Well, maybe they thought you were a bore.

FRANCIS: "Love enters through the eyes," that's Dante. . . .

JUDITH: And he liked little girls.

FRANCIS: Look, I don't know what you see when you look at me. I've made myself a monster—and tomorrow I'm to be twenty-one and all I can feel is myself sinking.

JUDITH: But, Francis . . .

FRANCIS: Look, I don't want to discuss it now, now here, not with my father around the corner. Now I'm going into my room and play some music. Then I'm going for a walk. I would appreciate it if you'd strike your tent and gather up your things and your brother and leave before I return.

[*He goes into his room and puts on some quiet music.* JUDITH *is left alone. Suddenly* RANDY *appears over the fence.*]

RANDY: This is very mysterious.

BLACKOUT

Scene 2

Scene the same. Later that day. It is early evening. During the scene, night falls.

FRAN *is cooking spaghetti in his kitchen. He is singing "Strangers in the Night."*

RANDY *is inside the tent.*

FRANCIS *enters through the gate. Sees the tent. He slams the gate.*

FRANCIS: They're still here.
FRAN: [*From inside house*] Yo, Francis, is that you?
FRANCIS: Yes.
FRAN: I'm in the kitchen.
   [FRANCIS *goes inside.*]
FRAN: Where have you been?
FRANCIS: Where is she now?
FRAN: In your room. Why don't you go in to see her?
FRANCIS: Didn't it ever occur to you that I don' want you to interfere . . . ?
FRAN: [*Smiles.*] "Strangers in the night . . ."
   [FRANCIS *goes into his room.* HERSCHEL *comes bounding in from the alley.*]
HERSCHEL: [*To* FRAN] Hi. Where's Randy?
FRAN: In his tent. [*Yells.*] Yo, Randy! You got company.
   [RANDY *peeks out of the tent.* HERSCHEL *sits down by the tent.*]
HERSCHEL: Hi. I just got back from my father's. He wanted me to stay over but I faked a petit mal and he let me go.
RANDY: A petit mal?
HERSCHEL: You know, a fit. A little one. I stumbled around and I slobbered and I told him everything was black. He got worried. I told him I left my medicine back here, so he gave me money for a cab. I took the bus.
   [FRANCIS *and* JUDITH *appear in window.*]

HERSCHEL: Like, I was wondering, would you like to come with me to, like, see the engine? It's not far from here. It's all right if you don't want to come, like, I mean, I understand, you know? Everybody can't be interested in public transportation, it's not that interesting, you know? So, like, I understand if you aren't interested but would you like to come?

RANDY: [*Who has gotten a towel and toilet case out of his knapsack*] Can we have dinner first?

HERSCHEL: You mean you'll come? How about that! I'll go and change—I'll be right back. [*He starts to run, trips over his own feet, falls, picks himself up, and runs into his house.*]

JUDITH: [*From window*] I see you're about to be broadened.

RANDY: What could I do? [*To* FRAN *in kitchen*] Mr. Geminiani!

FRAN: [*Appears in kitchen window.*] Fran, it's Fran!

RANDY: Fran. Can I take a shower?

FRAN: Be my guest. You got a towel?

RANDY: Yes. [*He goes into the house.*]

FRAN: [*Comes out, yelling.*] Yo, Francis!

FRANCIS: [*He and* JUDITH *are right behind him.*] Jesus Christ, I'm right here.

FRAN: That's my Ivy League son. Look, once in a while when your lips get tired, go in and stir the spaghettis, hanh? I'm going to get Lucille.

FRANCIS: She lives around the corner, why can't she come over herself?

FRAN: Don' get smart, and show some respect. She believes in the boogie man. [*He throws the kitchen towel in through the window, as if he were making a jump shot.*] Yes! Two points! [*Holds up two fingers like cuckold's horns.*] "Strangers in the night . . ." [*He exits through the gate.*]

JUDITH: Lucille and your father are—well, you know, aren't they?

FRANCIS: I don't know, they drink an awful lot of coffee.

JUDITH: Stimulates the gonads—[*She embraces* FRANCIS *and kisses him. He looks uncomfortable.*] What's the matter?

FRANCIS: I'm sorry.

JUDITH: Sorry about what?

[*He looks away.*]

JUDITH: You know, I think you are an eternal adolescent, a German Adolescent, a German Romantic Adolescent. You were born out of context, you'd have been much happier in the forties of the last century when it was eternally twilight.

FRANCIS: Do I detect a veiled reference to *Zwielicht* by Eichendorff?

JUDITH: I took Basic European Literature also, and did better than you did.

FRANCIS: You did not.

JUDITH: I got the highest mark on the objective test: 98! What did you get? [*She laughs.*]

FRANCIS: [*Bantering with her*] My SAT verbal and achievement tests were higher than yours.

JUDITH: How do you know?

FRANCIS: I looked them up in the office. I pretended to go faint, and while the registrar ran for water, I looked at your file.

JUDITH: [*Entering into his game*] I find that hard to believe; I had the highest score in the verbal at St. Paul's and also in the English Achievement Test.

FRANCIS: That's what it said alongside your IQ.

JUDITH: [*Taken aback in spite of herself*] My IQ?

FRANCIS: Very interesting, that IQ. It was recorded in bright red ink. There was also a parenthesis, in which someone had written: "Poor girl, but she has great determination."

JUDITH: I find jokes about IQ's in poor taste.

FRANCIS: Then you are an adolescent, a German Adolescent, a German Romantic Adolescent.

JUDITH: And before this edifying discussion you were about to say, "Fuck you, Judith."

FRANCIS: Don't put it that way. . . .

JUDITH: But more or less it was get lost, see you later, oh yes, have a nice summer—and maybe, just maybe, I'll tell you why later. You seem to want to skip that part, the why. [*She picks up the end of a garden hose, and points it at* FRANCIS *like a machine gun, and with a Humphrey Bogart voice, says:*] Look, I came to see you, that's ballsy, now you've got to reciprocate and tell me

why. . . . [*She puts down the hose, and the accent.*] Do
I bore you? Do you think I'm ugly? Do I have bad
breath?

FRANCIS: Oh, come on!

JUDITH: Hey, Francis, we're just alike, can't you see that?

FRANCIS: [*Indicates the house and yard.*] Oh yeah.

JUDITH: Two overachievers. Really. I know my family is
better off than yours; but we're just alike, and there
was something last winter and now you're telling me . . .

FRANCIS: Look, I'm going to be twenty-one tomorrow.
Well . . . I don't know what to say.

JUDITH: Is there a reason?

FRANCIS: I don't think I can say.

JUDITH: That doesn't make any sense.

FRANCIS: I think I'm. queer.

JUDITH: Why don't we back up a bit. I said, "We're just
alike et cetera," and you said you were going to be
twenty-one tomorrow, and I looked at you with deep-
set, sea-blue eyes, and you said . . .

FRANCIS: I think I'm queer.

JUDITH: [*Laughs.*] Well, I guess we can't get around it.
Do you want to amplify? I mean this seems like quite
a leap from what I remember of those long, sweet, ec-
static nights, naked in each other's young arms, cling-
ing to . . .

FRANCIS: We fucked. Big deal. That's what kids are supposed to do. And be serious.

JUDITH: I am serious. Is there a particular boy?

FRANCIS: Yes.

JUDITH: An adolescent, a German Adolescent . . .

FRANCIS: Not German, no.

JUDITH: Do I know him?

[FRANCIS *doesn't answer.*]

JUDITH: Reciprocal?

FRANCIS: It was just this spring. He began to haunt me.
We became friends. We talked a lot—late in my room
when you were studying. Well, I don't know, and you
see—I've had, well, crushes before. I dreamed of him.
It's not reciprocal, no, he doesn't know, but it became
more and more obvious to me. I mean, I'd look at him,
and then some other boy would catch my eye and I'd
think—you see?

JUDITH: Well. I suppose I could start teaching you the

secrets of makeup.

[FRANCIS *turns away, annoyed.*]

JUDITH: Well, how do you expect me to react? You seem
to think I ought to leap out the window because of it.
But it's like you're suddenly turning to me and saying
you are from Mars. Well, you might be, but I don't see
much evidence and I can't see what difference it
makes. I'm talking about you and me, I and thou and
all that. All right, maybe you do have an eye for the
boys, well, so do I, but you . . . you are special to me.
I wouldn't throw you over just because a hockey player
looked good, why do you have to give me up?

FRANCIS: I don't think that makes any sense, Judith. I
mean, if I were from Mars, it would make a difference,
I'd have seven legs and talk a different language and
that's how I feel now.

[JUDITH *embraces him.*]

FRANCIS: Don't touch me so much, Judith, and don't look
at me. . . .

JUDITH: Then you're afraid. That explains that fat and
ugly nonsense and this sudden homosexual panic.
You're afraid that anyone who responds to you will
make demands you can't meet. You're afraid you'll
fail. . . .

FRANCIS: Good Evening, Ladies and Gentlemen, Texaco
Presents: "Banality on Parade!"

JUDITH: You're afraid to venture. That's why you've en-
shrined someone who doesn't respond to you, probably
doesn't even know you're interested. If the relationship
never happens, you are never put to the test and can't
fail. The Overachiever's Great Nightmare!

FRANCIS: That's crazy!

JUDITH: I bet this boy who draws you is some Harvard
sprite, a dew-touched freshman. . . .

FRANCIS: He was a freshman.

JUDITH: In Randy's class and that proves it. Look at
Randy—what kind of response could someone like that
have but the giggles? And you know that. You're afraid
of commitment. And remember what Dante says about
those who refuse to make commitments. They're not
even in hell, but are condemned to run about the out-
skirts for eternity.

[FRANCIS, *who has heard enough, has stuck his head*

inside BUNNY's *kitchen window and brought it down over his neck like a guillotine.* JUDITH *now runs over to the fence and starts climbing to the top.*]

JUDITH: *Ed io che reguardai vidi una insegna che girando correva tanta ratta, che d'ogni posa me parea indegna* ... !

[*She leaps off the fence.* FRANCIS *runs to her aid.*]

FRANCIS: Judith! Jesus Christ!

JUDITH: [*As he helps her up*] You see? I ventured, I made the great leap and remained unscathed.

[HERSCHEL *runs out of his house, dressed in his old pants and torn sweat shirt, carrying one sneaker.*]

HERSCHEL: I heard a noise. Is Randy all right?

FRANCIS: Judith, you're all right?

JUDITH: Good as nude! [*Limps over to stoop and sits.*]

FRANCIS: Oh, shit! I forgot to stir the spaghetti. Now they'll all stick together.... [*Runs into the kitchen, runs out again.*] You're sure you're all right?

JUDITH: Stir the spaghetti. We don't want them sticking together.

[FRANCIS *goes into the kitchen.*]

HERSCHEL: You're the one who fell?

JUDITH: You might put it that way.

HERSCHEL: [*Sits down beside* JUDITH. *Puts on his other sneaker.*] I do that. One time I fell while I was having an asthma attack. My mother called the ambulance. She has, like, an uncle who's a driver. They rushed me to the hospital. Like, you know, the siren screaming? That was two years ago, right before I went to high school. It was St. Agnes Hospital over Track Thirty-seven on the A, the AA, the AA one through seven and the B express lines, maybe you passed it? I didn't get, like, hurt falling, you know. Still, my mother asked me what I wanted most in the whole world, you know? I told her and she let me ride the subway for twelve whole hours. Like, she rode them with me. She had to stay home from work for two days.

JUDITH: [*Crosses to tent, and gets a bandanna out of her knapsack. She sits down and starts cleaning her knee, which she'd hurt in leaping off the fence.*] Why are you so interested in the subways?

HERSCHEL: [*Joins her on the ground.*] Oh, not just the subways. I love buses too, you know? And my favorites are, well, you won't laugh? The trolleys. They are very beautiful. There's a trolley graveyard about two blocks from here. I was thinking, like maybe Randy would like to see that, you know? I could go see the engine anytime. The trolley graveyard is well, like, I guess, beautiful, you know? Really. They're just there, like old creatures everyone's forgotten, some of them rusted out, and some of them on their sides, and one, the old thirty-two, is like standing straight up as though sayin', like, I'm going to stand here and be myself, no matter what. I talk to them. Oh, I shouldn't have said that. Don't tell my mother, please? It's, you know, like people who go to castles and look for, for, well, like, knights in shining armor, you know? That past was beautiful and somehow, like, pure. The same is true of the trolleys. I follow the old thirty-two route all the time. It leads right to the graveyard where the thirty-two is buried, you know? It's like, well, fate. The tracks are half-covered with filth and pitch, new pitch like the city pours on. It oozes in the summer and people walk on it, but you can see the tracks and you see, like, it's true, like, old things last, good things last, like, you know? The trolleys are all filthy and half-covered and rusted out and laughed at, and even though they're not much use to anybody and kind of ugly like, by most standards, they're, like, they're, well, I guess, beautiful, you know?

[RANDY *enters, having finished his shower. He flicks his towel at* HERSCHEL.]

RANDY: Hey, that shower is a trip. I should have taken my surfboard.

HERSCHEL: Like, you should have used our shower, it's in much better shape, you know? Next time you want to take a shower, let me know.

JUDITH: Well, there's one cosmic issue settled.

RANDY: [*Crosses to kitchen window.*] Mmmmm. That sauce smells good.

FRANCIS: [*Appears in kitchen window.*] We call it gravy.

RANDY: When will it be ready?

FRANCIS: Soon. [*Disappears inside house.*]

HERSCHEL: [*To* RANDY] Then we can go to the graveyard. [RANDY *looks surprised.*]

HERSCHEL: See, like, I decided it might be, well, more

fun, if we saw all the dead trolleys, you know, and leave the engine for later.

RANDY: Whatever you say. [*Back to the window.*] Francis, look—is there something wrong?

FRAN: [*Offstage, yelling*] Yo, Francis! We're here. [*Comes in from gate.*] Hi, kids. [*Going into house*] You stir that stuff?

FRANCIS: [*From inside*] Yeah.

[RANDY *gets a shirt out of his knapsack and crawls into the tent.* HERSCHEL *starts crawling into the tent.*]

RANDY: Herschel . . . careful!

HERSCHEL: [*Inside the tent*] I'm careful.

LUCILLE: [*Offstage*] Judith!

RANDY: Well, sit over there.

[HERSCHEL *plops down, blocking the entire entrance with his back.* LUCILLE *comes into the yard with a sweater and jacket. She approaches* JUDITH.]

LUCILLE: Judy, I brought you a sweater. I thought you might be chilly later tonight and I didn't know if you brought one with you.

JUDITH: Thank you.

LUCILLE: [*Puts sweater around* JUDITH'S *shoulders.*] It's real sheep's wool. My friend Diane gave it to me. Her daughter, Joann, is a model for KYZ-TV in Center City—special shift. She's a Cancer, so am I, that's why Fran says I'm a disease. My son, Donny, he's at Yale in pre-med, Branford scholarship, I think he'll make a wonderful doctor, don't Yale make wonderful doctors?

JUDITH: I'm sure I don't know.

[FRAN *comes out with* FRANCIS. *He is carrying a large fold-up metal table.*]

FRAN: Make yourself useful, Lucille. I got the table, go get the plates.

RANDY: [*Getting away from* HERSCHEL, *who is hovering around him*] I'll help set up.

[LUCILLE *goes into the house, and returns with a tray, with plates, napkins, cutlery, glasses, bug spray, and a "plastic lace" tablecloth.*]

FRAN: How was your shower?

RANDY: I expected to see seals and Eskimos any minute.

FRAN: At least you got out of the bathroom alive. There are beach chairs in the cellar, why don't you get them?

Francis, show this young man where the beach chairs is in the cellar.

[FRAN *goes back into house*, FRANCIS, RANDY, *and* HERSCHEL *go past the house to the cellar, and* LUCILLE *starts setting the table.*]

LUCILLE: You know Judy, my daughter, she's a dental technician at the Graduate Hospital—special shift. She wanted to go to Yale, but she couldn't get in. She thought it was her teeth. They're buck. She said the woman looked at her funny the whole time at the interview. Now I told her she should just carry herself with poise and forget her teeth. Y'know what she said to me: How can I forget my teeth; they're in my mouth! Not a very poised thing to say. That's why she didn't get into Yale: No poise. That's why she ain't got no husband, either. Do the people at Yale think teeth are important?

JUDITH: I don't know anything about Yale.

LUCILLE: But what do you think?

JUDITH: Yes, I think teeth are very important for success in life. [*She is setting out cutlery.*] At the prep school I attended they had us practice our bite three times a day.

LUCILLE: [*Politely, taken in*] Oh?

JUDITH: We would bite off a poised bite, and chew with poise, and then sing a C major scale whilst we swilled the food in our mouths. I could even sing songs whilst swilling food with poise. In fact, I once sang the first aria of the Queen of the Night while swilling half a hamburger and a bucket of french fries. . . . Of course, remaining utterly poised, or "pwased," as we say at Harvard.

LUCILLE: Oh. [*She walks around the table spraying insect repellant.*] It kills them very quickly.

[FRANCIS, RANDY, *and* HERSCHEL *enter the yard with beach chairs and old kitchen chairs, which they proceed to set up.*]

RANDY: [*To* FRANCIS, *continuing a conversation*] C'mon, Francis, what's going on?

FRAN: [*From the kitchen*] Yo, Lucille, give me a hand!

JUDITH: I'll be glad to help. [*Runs into the kitchen.*]

RANDY: Come on, Francis, I mean I'm three years younger than you—so tell me . . .

[*Simultaneously,* LUCILLE *and* HERSCHEL *approach* RANDY.]

HERSCHEL: Would you like to see my models of the trolley fleet of 1926?

LUCILLE: [*Giving* RANDY *a jacket*] I brought you one of my son's jackets, because I thought you might get cold later and I didn't know if you brought one wit you. My son's girl friend bought it for him at Wanamaker's.

[FRAN *and* JUDITH *come back out.*]

BUNNY: [*Calling from inside her house*] Yo! Where is everybody?

FRAN: Yo, Bun! We're out here.

[BUNNY *comes stumbling out of her house. She has been drinking. She never stops moving, constantly dancing and leaping about, she cries out in war whoops and screams of victory.*]

BUNNY: I won! I won! I wanna kiss from everybody but Lucille! [*She goes around kissing everyone, except* LU-CILLE. *She gets to* RANDY.] Oh, you're such a honey bun, I could eat you. [*She kisses him, then grabs his crotch.*] I'll skip Francis, too.

RANDY: Wanna smoke, Herschel?

HERSCHEL: Sure.

[*They sit down by the tent,* HERSCHEL *sitting as far away from* BUNNY *as possible.*]

BUNNY: Break out the horse piss, Fran!

[FRAN *goes into the kitchen for liquor.*]

BUNNY: Jesus Christ in Heaven, I won!

FRAN: [*Returns with a bottle of scotch.*] How do you want it?

BUNNY: Straight up the dark and narrow path, honey. [*She takes a swig from the bottle.*] You shoulda seen me in that courtroom, I told them all about it, that bitch didn't even have the decency to fart before throwin' herself on top a me. I coulda been ruptured for life, I says, and she's a Catholic, I couldn't believe it. Catholics got self-control.

LUCILLE: [*To* JUDITH] Well, good Catholics have self-control. Sister Mary Emaryd, my friend, she used to work at Wanamaker's before she married Christ. She . . .

BUNNY: [*To* RANDY] That judge looked at me, let me tell you.

LUCILLE: She would allow herself to go to the bathroom only twice a day.

BUNNY: [*To* FRAN] I felt twenty again.

LUCILLE: [*To* JUDITH] She said: Urgency is all in the mind.

BUNNY: [*To* RANDY] I felt like a fuckin' young filly in heat. Look, honey, you ever see my boobies swayin'? [*She sways them for* RANDY. *He giggles.*]

LUCILLE: [*To* FRANCIS] I go to the bathroom more than that, yet I go to Mass every Sunday. . . .

BUNNY: [*To* RANDY] You smokin' that killer weed, hon?

RANDY: Sure. You want some?

BUNNY: Don' need that shit. Don' need nothin' to get high, I'm high naturally. I was born floatin'. [*She leans on table, almost knocking everything over.*] Come and dance with me, baby. [*She grabs a very reluctant* RANDY.] C'mon! "Flat foot floozie with the floy, floy . . ." [*They start doing the jitterbug, and* RANDY *bumps into* BUNNY, *knocking the breath out of her.*]

BUNNY: Fuck you, world! Fuck you, Mary O'Donnel! Fuck you, Sam the Jew! Fuck you, Catholic Church! Fuck you, Mom! I won! You shoulda seen them look at me, I felt like a fuckin' starlit. My boobies swayin', and when I walked to the stand I did my strut, my fuckin' bitch-in-heat strut. Come on, Lucille, can you strut like this? [*She comes up behind* LUCILLE *and "bumps" her.* LUCILLE *starts swearing in Italian.* BUNNY *turns to* JUDITH.] Come on, honey, what's your name, can you strut like this? I can fuckin' strut up a storm. My hips have made many a wave in their time, honey, many a wave! I sent out hurricanes, I sent out earthquakes, I sent out tidal waves from my fuckin' hips. Yo, Fran!

FRAN: Yo, Bun!

BUNNY: Remember when I was in that fuckin' community theater down at Gruen Recreation Center?

FRAN: Seventeenth Street.

LUCILLE: Sixteenth and Wolf!

BUNNY: I played Sadie Thompson in that play. I let my hair grow down long. It was real long then, not dyed shit yellow like it is now. I fuckin' got hair like hepatitis now. I played that part! I hadda sheer slip on and my legs, Jesus Christ, my legs! I fuckin' felt the earth trem-

ble when I walked, I played that bitch like Mount Ve-
suvius and the clappin', honey, the clappin'!

FRAN: You were a big hit, yep.

BUNNY: At the curtain call, I held my boobs out like this:
[*She sticks out her chest.*] . . . and they screamed,
honey, those fuckin' grown men screamed! [*To* RANDY]
Feel 'em, honey, feel these grapes of mine. [*She puts*
RANDY's *hand on her boobs.*]

RANDY: Mrs. Weinberger!

BUNNY: They're still nice, hanh? I fuckin' won that case!
[*She has to sit down.*] Then I married Sam the Jew and
bore Herschel. Look at the fruit of my loins, look, this
is one of the earthquakes I sent out of my hips. Boom!
Boom! When he walks you can hear him around the
corner, but he's a fuckin' genius at least. He's got an
IQ of 187 or 172, dependin' on which test you use,
despite his father!

LUCILLE: [*This has been building up.*] Che disgraziat'!
[*She runs into the house, followed by* FRAN.]

BUNNY: [*Looking after* FRAN] I coulda had . . . well, almost anybody, more or less. I coulda been a chorus girl,
then I met Sam the Kike and that was that. He had the
evil eye, that Hebe, them little pointy eyes. He'd screw
them up like he was lookin' for blackheads, then, suddenly, they'd go real soft and get big. I was a sucker
for them fuckin' eyes. He's a jeweler, called me his
jewel. Sam the Jew. I smell like old peanuts!

RANDY: [*Offering her the joint*] Sure you don't want
some?

BUNNY: No, honey, I got me some coke for a giddy sniff.
I get it from my uncle on the force; he gives me a
discount, he's a captain. [*She suddenly sees* HERSCHEL
smoking behind the tent.] Hey, wait a minute! You
been smokin' that shit? Herschel! Have you been
smokin' that shit?

HERSCHEL: [*Butts the joint quickly.*] No . . .

BUNNY: Don' you lie to me. Didn't I tell you never to
smoke that shit? It'll fuckin' rot your brain and you'll
be more of a vegetable than you already are. God damn
you, I'll beat the shit outa you! [*She lunges for him.*]

HERSCHEL: [*Scurrying out of her way*] Come on!

BUNNY: Come on?? Come on??? I'll come on, you fuckin'
four-eyed fat-assed creep, I'll come on!

[*She grabs the bottle of scotch and chases* HERSCHEL *into the house. We see them in their kitchen window. She is beating the shit out of* HERSCHEL.]

BUNNY: Twelve fuckin' hours! Twelve fuckin' hours I was in labor wit you, screamin' on that table, and for what? To fuckin' find you smokin' dope? [*His asthma attack is starting.*] That's right! Go ahead! Have a fuckin' asthma attack, cough your fuckin' head off! See if I care! [*She disappears inside the house.* HERSCHEL *is at the window, gasping for air, until he realizes that she has gone. His asthma attack miraculously stops. He disappears. During* HERSCHEL's *attack everyone onstage stares at him, horrified.* RANDY *passes* JUDITH *the joint. She refuses it.* FRANCIS *takes a toke, and passes it back to* RANDY. BUNNY, *inside her house, is heard singing at the out-of-tune piano, offstage.*]

BUNNY: "Moon river, wider than a mile,
   I'm screwing up in style someday. . . ."
[FRAN *and* LUCILLE *come in from the house. He has a big bowl of spaghetti, and she is carrying a very elaborate antipasto.*]

FRAN: [*Sitting down at the head of the table*] Well, I hope everybody's gotta appetite, 'cause there's enough to feed the Chinee army and ain't no room to keep it either.

LUCILLE: [*Sniffing the air*] I think the Delassandros down the alley are burning their children's clothing again. That smell!
[RANDY *and* FRANCIS *break up, and put out the joint.*]

FRAN: You all got plates, I'll serve. Francis, you get the gravy pot, I'll pass the macs, we also got antipast'; made special by Lucille Pompi . . . [LUCILLE *simpers.*] . . . and Lucille Pompi's antipast' is a delicacy.
[*He gives* LUCILLE *a hug.* FRANCIS *arrives with the gravy pot.* FRAN *is serving.*]

FRAN: And here we got the gravy meat: veal, sausage, lamb, meatballs, and braciole. [*He passes plate to* JUDITH.]

JUDITH: Oh, that's too much!

FRAN: Your stomach's bigger than your eyes. We also got wine. Francis!
[RANDY *snaps his fingers at* FRANCIS, *as if to say: Hop*

to it. FRANCIS *goes into house for wine.* FRAN *passes plate to* LUCILLE.]

FRAN: Lucille?

LUCILLE: No thank you, Fran, I'll just pick.

FRAN: [*Passes the plate to* RANDY.] Randy?

[LUCILLE *is busy making sure everyone is taken care of.* FRANCIS *has returned and is going around the table pouring wine.* FRAN *serves a plate to* FRANCIS.]

FRAN: Francis?

FRANCIS: I'm not so hungry tonight.

FRAN: [*Keeping the plate for himself*] Oh, we better get down on our knees, we've just witnessed a miracle.

LUCILLE: Oh, Fran, don't blaspheme.

FRAN: [*Everyone is eating but* LUCILLE.] Sure you don' wan' none, Lucille?

LUCILLE: I'll just pick out of your plate. [*She then proceeds to pick a large piece of lettuce from* FRAN's *plate and stuffs it in her mouth.*]

FRAN: [*To* RANDY *and* JUDITH] You kids enjoying your stay?

[LUCILLE *now gets a forkful of spaghetti from* FRAN's *plate and proceeds to eat that.*]

FRAN: This is your first time in South Philly, I bet. You ought to get Francis to take you around tomorrow and see the sights. Them sights'll make you nearsighted, that's how pretty South Philly is.

[LUCILLE *has speared more lettuce from* FRAN, *and he grabs her wrist.*]

FRAN: Yo, Lucille, I'll get you a plate.

LUCILLE: [*She frees her hand, stuffs the lettuce in her mouth, and says:*] No, thank you, Fran, I'm not hungry. [*She notices something on* JUDITH's *plate, picks it, and eats it.* JUDITH *and* RANDY *are amazed.*]

FRAN: Lucille! Let that kid alone and fill your own plate.

LUCILLE: [*With a full mouth*] Fran, I'm not hungry! [*She sees a tomato wedge on* RANDY's *plate. She picks up her fork, and pounces on the tomato.*]

FRAN: Lucille!

LUCILLE: He wasn't going to eat that.

FRAN: How do you know?

LUCILLE: Look how skinny he is.

[HERSCHEL *appears in his doorway.*]

FRAN: Hi ya, Herschel.
[*Everyone greets him.*]
FRAN: You feel better?
HERSCHEL: I guess.
FRAN: Well, get a plate and sit down!
HERSCHEL: You don't mind?
FRAN: You're the guest of honor.
[HERSCHEL *comes down to the table, to the empty chair, and starts pulling it around the table, making* FRANCIS *get out of the way, until he is next to* RANDY. RANDY, JUDITH, *and* LUCILLE, *who are all sitting on the long side of the table, have to scoot over to make room for* HERSCHEL. *He sits down next to* RANDY.]
HERSCHEL: [*To* RANDY] Can we still . . .
RANDY: Yeah, yeah, sure.
[FRAN *has piled spaghetti and sauce for* HERSCHEL. *He is trying to pass the plate down to* HERSCHEL, *but* LUCILLE *snatches it, gets a forkful of pasta, and then passes the plate on. Everyone except* FRANCIS *is eating.*]
FRAN: Gonna be night soon. And tomorrow's my son's birthday. Seems like yesterday he was my little buddy, on the chubby side, but cute all the same, and tomorrow he's gonna be—what? Six? Gonna be a man tomorrow. Looka him squirm. Everybody hits twenty-one sooner or later, 'cept me, I'm still nineteen. *Salute!*
[*They all lift their glasses in a toast and drink, except* HERSCHEL, *who keeps shoveling it down.*]
FRAN: Judith, look, you can see that fig tree wave in the wind if you squint. Francis, remember the day I planted it? I got the sledgehammer out of the cellar, people that was here before us left it, and I broke that concrete. His mother, she'd had enough of both of us, and took off, headin' down South. She was like a bird had too much of winter. Met a nice southern man.
LUCILLE: Protestant.
FRAN: They're married. Can't have kids, though; she had a hysterectomy just before she left. It's a shame. She's good people and so's this man, she should had kids wit him. He's real normal, nice-lookin', don' cough like I do, don' get rashes neither, and to him, horses is for ridin'!

[*He breaks himself up. Then starts to cough.* LUCILLE *is picking out of* JUDITH's *plate. Big forkful of spaghetti.*]

FRAN: They'd have had nice kids. The kind that woulda made her happy. She's one of them people that like to fade inna the air. Don' wanna stand out. Francis and me, well, we stand out. Don' wanna, understand, but we talk too loud, cough, scratch ourselves, get rashes, are kinda big. You have to notice us. Don' have to like us but you gotta see us.

[LUCILLE *pats* FRAN's *cheek lovingly.*]

FRAN: Well, his mother, she was good people and meant well, but she wasn't too easy wit us, she wanted a home in the suburbs, all the Sears and Roebuck catalogs lined up against the wall, and two white kids, just like her, white like the fog, kids you hadda squint to see. Well, this one day, she packed her bags, see, rented a big truck and took everything, even my portable TV. [*He laughs at the "joke."*] I guess it'll be cool tonight. She left me, you see, she left me. So I come out here and smash that concrete. Next day I planted the fig tree. I went to the one guy in the neighborhood would give me the time of day, borrowed thirty dollars, and bought this tree, the dirt, some fertilizer. . . .

[LUCILLE's *hand is in his plate again.*]

FRAN: Jesus Christ in Heaven! Lucille! Would you fill your own plate and stop actin' like the poor relative?!

LUCILLE: [*Quickly stuffs food in her mouth.*] Stop pickin' on me! I ain't actin' like the poor relative!

FRAN: Whataya call pickin' at his plate, then pickin' at my plate, then pickin' at his plate, then pickin' at her plate, for Christ' sake, hanh? Stop pickin'! Take! Take wit both hands, it's there, why you act like there ain't plenty when there is, hanh? What's the matter you???!!!! [*He has taken two enormous handfuls of spaghetti out of the bowl and dropped them into* LUCILLE's *plate.*]

LUCILLE: [*Screaming*] Eh! Sta'zit'!

FRAN: [*Shaking her plate under her nose*] Mangi taci' o—

LUCILLE: [*Stands up and screams at him.*] Fongoul! [*She runs out of the yard.*]

FRAN: Jesus Christ! See you kids later. [*Yells.*] Lucille, I was only kidding! [*Runs off after her.*]

HERSCHEL: [*Rising, to* RANDY] I'm finished,
RANDY: [*With a sigh*] All right. [*To* JUDITH *and* FRANCIS]
See you later.
[HERSCHEL *and* RANDY *exit through the alley.*]
JUDITH: [*Rises, starts stacking.*] I'll put the dishes in the
sink. [*She suddenly drops the plates on the table.*] It's
Randy, isn't it?
BUNNY: [*Stumbles out of her house. She is in her robe
and nightgown again.*] Hi, you two. You got some more
horse piss? I'm out.
FRANCIS: I'll look, Bunny. [*Runs into his kitchen.*]
BUNNY: You look sort of peaked, hon, upset over some-
thin'? A man, maybe?
JUDITH: Maybe.
BUNNY: Well, take my advice and heat up the coke bottle;
men ain't worth shit, not shit.
FRANCIS [*Coming out with a bottle*] Here, Bunny,
BUNNY: [*Takes a slug of whiskey.*] You're a saint, just a
fuckin' saint.
[*She collapses in a heap, completely out.* FRANCIS *gets
her under each arm, and* JUDITH *holds the door open.*
FRANCIS *starts dragging her back in.*]
BUNNY: [*Coming to for a moment*] Shit! Why am I such
a whale? Why ain't I a porpoise or a dolphin? Why do
I gotta be a whale wit hepatitis hair?
FRANCIS: Come on, Bunny, I'll help you inside. . . .
BUNNY: You're a saint, a fuckin' saint.
[*They disappear inside* BUNNY's *house.* FRANCIS *re-
turns immediately.*]
JUDITH: You and Randy. . . !
FRANCIS: Me and Randy nothing. He doesn't know a
thing about it. He's been following me around all day
asking why I won't look at him. What can I say? We
were friends, and he can't understand. . . .
[RANDY *and* HERSCHEL *have reentered from the al-
ley.*]
FRANCIS: Well, who can understand. . . .
JUDITH: What about the trolleys?
HERSCHEL: A different guard was there. We can go to-
morrow though, my friend'll be there.
RANDY: [*To* JUDITH] What's the matter?
JUDITH: [*To* FRANCIS, *indicating* RANDY] Just look at him.
[*Peals of laughter.*] And look at you.

HERSCHEL: [*To* RANDY] It's early yet, would you like to see my books on ornamental tiles. . . .

RANDY: Good night, Herschel.

HERSCHEL: I guess everybody can't be interested in . . .

RANDY: [*Pushes him inside, and closes the door behind him.*] Good night, Herschel!

HERSCHEL: Good night, Randy. [*Disappears inside his house.*]

RANDY: [*To* FRANCIS *and* JUDITH] Now, what's going on? [JUDITH *continues laughing.*]

RANDY: Francis?

FRANCIS: All right, Judith, why don't you just tell him?

JUDITH: And you don't want him told? What future is there for you if he doesn't even know? Happiness begins with knowledge, doesn't it?

FRANCIS: If it does, you are in a lot of trouble! [*Runs into his house, slamming the door.*]

RANDY: Hey, look, this is unfair. What's going on?

JUDITH: I have discovered this fine day that I have a rival for the affections of one Francis Geminiani.

RANDY: Oh yeah? I'm not surprised.

JUDITH: What?

RANDY: Well, Judy, you're kind of a bitch, you know. I mean, talking in Italian to his father and Lucille—nothing personal, I mean. . . .

JUDITH: Well, you are a creep, aren't you?

RANDY: And I mean like forcing me to look at those subway books with Herschel, just so you could be alone with Francis. So who's this rival? Somebody from the neighborhood who can make good gravy? [*He is laughing, and crawling inside the tent.*]

JUDITH: [*Starts rubbing her hands together gleefully.*] Well, the person in question is in the yard right now, under the fig tree, and it isn't me.

RANDY: [*Pops his head out.*] What?

BLACKOUT

ACT II

Scene 1

Scene the same. The next morning, about nine o'clock.

As the lights come up, FRANCIS *is seen in his window, staring at the tent.* JUDITH *is asleep in a sleeping bag outside the tent, and* RANDY *is inside.*

BUNNY *comes out of her house, dressed in her ragged housecoat; she is disoriented and mumbles to herself.* FRANCIS *sees her but says nothing.*

She is carrying a brown paper bag. She disappears into the alley, and is next seen climbing up the telephone pole behind the alley wall. She has to stop every few rungs and almost falls off once or twice. Finally she gets to the top of the alley wall, still clutching the bag, shakes her fist at the heavens, and prepares to jump.

A dog is heard barking in the distance.

FRANCIS: [*Yelling from his window*] Hey, Bunny! What are you doing?
BUNNY: [*Peering in his direction, trying to bring him into focus*] Hanh?
FRANCIS: What are you doing?
BUNNY: Who's 'at?
FRANCIS: Francis next door. Come down, you'll hurt yourself.
BUNNY: What are ya, blind? You go to Harvard and can't tell I'm gonna jump?
FRANCIS: Bunny!
BUNNY: Shut up, Francis, I'm gonna splatter my fuckin'

body on the concrete down there and don' wan' no interference. I thought it all out. My uncle's an under-taker, he'll do it cheap..

[HERSCHEL *sticks his head out the second-story win-dow of* BUNNY'*s house.*]

HERSCHEL: Mom! What are you doing?

BUNNY: Herschel, don' look, it'll give you asthma.

HERSCHEL: Don't jump, Mom!

BUNNY: Herschel, I gotta favor to ask of you. If I don' die in jumpin', I want you to finish me off wit this. [*Waves the bag.*] It's rat poison. Was Uncle Eddie's Christmas present.

HERSCHEL: Mom, please!

BUNNY: You didn't scratch them new mosquito bites, did you?

HERSCHEL: No. And I took my medicine and I used my atomizer and brushed my teeth, please don't jump.

BUNNY: Good, you keep it up. Don' wan' to be a mess at my funeral.

HERSCHEL: Funeral!

[*Pulls his head in, and runs out into the yard.* JUDITH *is awake and getting dressed.* RANDY *comes out of the tent, a little confused by the noise.* FRANCIS *has come out and is trying to coax her down.*]

RANDY: What's going on?

HERSCHEL: [*Arrives, puffing, in the yard. His pajamas are disgracefully dirty, as is his robe, which is much too small for him.*] Please, Mom, I'm sorry, I didn't mean to do it. . . .

BUNNY: What?

HERSCHEL: I don't know, it must be something I did. I'll never have asthma again, I'll stop having seizures, I'll take gym class. Don't jump!

BUNNY: [*Starts climbing higher, until she is about the height of the second-story window.*] Herschel, is that any way to act, hanh? Was you raised in the jungle? Show some dignity, you want the neighbors to talk?

HERSCHEL: I'll burn my transfer collection, I'll give up the subways. . . .

BUNNY: Nah, that's all right, Herschel. You'll be better off in a home.

HERSCHEL: A home??!!! [*He can hardly get the word out. He starts having an asthma attack.*]

BUNNY: Jesus Christ in heaven, he's havin' an attack! Can't I even commit suicide in peace?

JUDITH: Should I call the police?

FRANCIS: Call Lucille. DE 6-1567.

JUDITH: DE 6-1567. [*She runs into* FRANCIS's *house.*]

RANDY: What about Herschel?

BUNNY: Get his fuckin' atomizer—it's in the third room on the second floor.

[RANDY *runs into* BUNNY's *house.*]

BUNNY: Jesus Christ in heaven! And it's all for attention.

FRANCIS: What is, Bunny?

BUNNY: His fuckin' attacks! I read them books! It's all for attention, that all these kids want nowadays. I didn't get no attention when I was a kid and look at me! Am I weird? Nah! I didn't get no asthma, I didn't even get pimples.

JUDITH: [*Appears in the kitchen window.*] I get a busy signal.

FRANCIS: Busy? This time of day?

BUNNY: They think because they can fart and blink at the same time they got the world conquered.

FRANCIS: Did you get the number right?

BUNNY: That's all they want: attention!

JUDITH: DE 6-1567.

FRANCIS: Jesus! That's our number. It's DE 6-1656.

[JUDITH *disappears inside the house.* RANDY *appears in the second-story window of* BUNNY's *house.*]

RANDY: I can't find the atomizer!

HERSCHEL: [*Gasping, on the ground at the foot of the wall*] By the bed, under all the Kleenex!

[RANDY *continues looking for it.*]

FRANCIS: Come on, Bunny, climb down!

BUNNY: [*Climbing down to the top of the wall*] Education! That's these kids' problems! Look at him—a fuckin' genius; and he looks like some live turd some fuckin' giant laid. Huff some more, Herschel. . . .

RANDY: [*Running out of house*] I got it! I got it!

[HERSCHEL *grabs the atomizer. His attack subsides.*]

BUNNY: They all oughtta be put to work! That's what happened to me. Yeah! My mom put me to work when I was ten, singin' songs for pennies in the Franciscan monastery on Wolf Street!

[JUDITH *comes back into the yard.*]

BUNNY: I hadda sing for everybody—them bums, them old ladies. Once some crazy old lady made me sing "Mein Yiddische Mama" six times—then gave me a five-dollar bill. Well, even though it's a Catholic place I figured, shit, make the money. So I learned ".Bei Mir Bist Du Shoen" for the next week and sang it—and they beat the shit outa me. If that wasn't a birth trauma, what was! I read them books, know all about it. I've hadda shit-filled life; feel like some turd stuck in the pipe so Herschel get your fat ass outa the way, you too, hon, or I'll crush youse!

FRAN: [*Offstage, yelling*] What's goin' on out here?

BUNNY: Yo, Fran!

FRAN: Yo, Bun!

BUNNY: I'm gonna jump!

LUCILLE: [*Running into the yard from gate, in hair curlers*] *Che disgraziat'!* Who's gonna clean it up, hanh?

FRAN: [*Follows* LUCILLE *in.*] Whataya mean you're gonna jump?

BUNNY: Whataya mean, whataya mean? I'm gonna leap off this fuckin' wall and if that don' finish me I'm takin' this rat poison and Herschel better move or I'm takin' him with me. Jesus Christ, can't even die without his havin' a attack.

[FRAN *and* FRANCIS *half-carry, half-drag* HERSCHEL *away from the wall and lay him down on the stoop. He is screaming and kicking.*]

BUNNY: You mean I gotta listen to that in heaven?

LUCILLE: You ain't going to heaven!

FRAN: Come on, be good and get down. You don't got no reason to jump!

BUNNY: I got reason, I got reason!

FRAN: Yeah, what?

BUNNY: Got nobody in the whole fuckin' world, I turned ugly, I got no money, I ain't got no prospects. . . .

FRAN: That's been true of my whole life and you don' see me jumpin' off alley walls and takin' rat poison. Besides, it's Francis's twenty-first birthday today.

BUNNY: You mean there's gonna be a party?

FRAN: A big one!

BUNNY: Why didn't you say so, hanh? Get that friggin' ladder, I'm comin' down!

[FRANCIS *and* RANDY *run to get the ladder that has*

been leaning against the fence. They set it up under
the wall and help BUNNY *climb down.*]
BUNNY: [*To* RANDY] You're so strong, hon, give me a kiss!
[*Kisses him. Then she turns on* HERSCHEL, *who is still*
wheezing and crying.] You! Get in that fuckin' house!
Makin' a spectacle of yourself wit them pajamas!
[*She chases* HERSCHEL *into their house. Much shaking*
of heads from the others. Everyone is very tense. FRAN-
CIS *takes the ladder back to the fence.*]
HERSCHEL: [*As he is running inside*] What the fuck do
you want me to do?
BUNNY: [*In her house, continuing a diatribe against* HER-
SCHEL] And what's this I hear from your no-good
father? You had a fuckin' petit mal yesterday?!
HERSCHEL: [*In the house*] No I didn't!
BUNNY: Liar! Didn't I tell you to behave wit him?
[*Sounds of her beating him.*] I told you to act nor-
mal.
HERSCHEL: Who could act normal with you for a mother?
[*A sound like a piano falling over is heard from*
BUNNY's *house. A silence. Then suddenly, long sur-*
prised screams of pain from HERSCHEL. FRAN *tries to*
hug FRANCIS. FRANCIS *gets away.* BUNNY *comes run-*
ning out of her house to the stoop.]
BUNNY: You guys wanna get a piano offa Herschel?
FRAN: What's the piano doin' on Herschel?
BUNNY: He gave me some lip and I threw it on him.
FRAN: Oh, all right. [*Kisses* FRANCIS.] Happy birthday,
my son.
[FRAN *and* FRANCIS *run into* BUNNY's *house.*]
BUNNY: Do you think I ruptured him for life?
[BUNNY *and* RANDY *run into the house.* JUDITH *begins*
to follow, but LUCILLE *stops her.*]
LUCILLE: Ain't ladylike to go in there.
JUDITH: Herschel might be hurt.
LUCILLE: If that kid ain't dead yet, he's indestructible.
[*From inside the house, noises of the piano being*
lifted.] He's always fallin' down stairs, gettin' hit by
cars, gettin' beat up, havin' fits, gettin' asthma, throwin'
up, comin' down with pneumonia. A piano ain't gonna
hurt him. [*She sets a garden chair next to the tent.*]
Besides, that piano's out of tune, how much damage
could it do?

JUDITH: This is crazy! All that noise and Bunny on the wall . . .

LUCILLE: [*Sits in chair.*] Happens alla the time. That's why no neighbors stuck their heads out. We're used to it around here. Tessie across the street come back from the shore last Sunday and found this burglar in her cellar.

[JUDITH *has gone in the tent to finish dressing.*]

LUCILLE: Judy, she ties him to an old sofa, then, wit her sister, she shoves it down the front steps. Then she sets it on fire. We come back from church and there is this sofa on the front steps wit a screamin' man on it and flames everywhere. We call the fire engine. They hose the poor bastard down and rush him to the hospital. So this mornin' was mild, believe me.

[JUDITH *is now sitting by the tent, putting on her sneakers.*]

LUCILLE: Do you wanna come wit me to Wanamaker's and buy Francis a present? I have a employee's discount so you can buy him somethin' real nice for less. Or did you get somethin' already?

JUDITH: Not really—a few joke things. I don't think he's gonna think they're funny.

[*She gets a brush and mirror out of her knapsack. Music is heard from* BUNNY'S *house.* BUNNY *appears in her window, brushing her hair.*]

BUNNY: Yo, Lucille! We got the piano up. You wanna come in and sing?

LUCILLE: No, Bunny.

BUNNY: Well, I'm cookin' breakfast. You wan' some?

LUCILLE and JUDITH: No thanks.

JUDITH: How is Herschel?

BUNNY: A little purple about the shins, but he'll survive. You sure you don' wan' some breakfast?

JUDITH: No thank you!

BUNNY: You should take some lessons from your brother. [*She disappears inside her house.*]

LUCILLE: What did she mean about your brother?

JUDITH: Everybody loves Randy—EVERYBODY it seems!

LUCILLE: Well, he's nice-lookin', that's for sure. But I'm not crazy about him. I never warm up to white people much. You're an exception. You got poise. You have lovely teeth.

[*From inside the house we hear:*]
"I want a girl
Just like the girl
That married dear old Dad,
She was a pearl
And the only girl
That Daddy ever had. . . ."
[*Dialogue continues over this.*]

JUDITH: They got Francis to play the piano, all those wrong notes.

LUCILLE: Why are you interested in Francis when you're so beautiful?

JUDITH: If I hear that once more, I'm going to stick my face in acid!

LUCILLE: But why? *Perchè?* What do you see in him?

JUDITH: Why are you interested in his father?

LUCILLE: I ain't got much choice. I'm not pretty. I'm a widow. Nobody wants a widow. It's like bein' an old sheet. I might be clean and kept nice, but people can't help noticin' it's been used.

[BUNNY *is heard singing* "When Irish eyes are smilin'."]

LUCILLE: [*Continues over song.*] So I put up with Fran. He's good people, he means well. But you know, he coughs alla the time, eats too much, makes noises, you know he's got the colitis, and them rashes! Between coughin', scratchin', and runnin' to the bathroom, I'm surprised he's got so much weight on him. Oh, well, that's my life.

[JUDITH *offers her the brush. She is about to use it, then discreetly pulls* JUDITH's *hair out of the bristles.*]

LUCILLE: But, Francis? Like father like son, remember.

JUDITH: Oh, I don't know. We talked yesterday and I was up most of the night, thinking: why? All the possible bad reasons started cramming themselves into my head. Perhaps I have sensed it all along and I was attracted to Francis because he was . . . [*Stops herself.*] Well, just because he's the way he is.

[*From inside the house we hear:*]
"For it was Mary, Mary,
Plain as any name can be,
For in society, propriety
Will say, Marie."

LUCILLE: [*Speaks over this.*] You mean queer? Don't be

shocked, I know what queer is. [*She turns her chair toward* JUDITH.] I had a long talk wit my son, Donny, about it before he went off. He's at Yale, pre-med, Branford scholarship. I warned him to be careful. My friend Diane's husband, he's a foot doctor, they met in a singles bar, then got married because he had corns real bad, well, he told me, Yale puts out a lot of queers along wit the doctors and the lawyers. But Donny's got a girl friend, and though I think she's a pig, I guess it proves he's got some interest in the girls. But Francis? Well, Fran and me had a long talk. He's afraid for Francis. Well, I think Francis is. There ain't been no girls around here except to sell cookies. That's why Fran was so happy to see you, and wanted you to stay, even though you wanted to go. It's hard on a man to have a queer for a son. I mean, I guess Fran would rather he was queer than humpbacked or dead, still it's hard.

JUDITH: Well, I thought that might be why I was interested. He'd be safe then. But I don't think so. He and I are really alike, you see. Neither of us makes contact with people. We both goof a lot, but most of the time, that's all there is.

BUNNY: [*From inside her house*] All right, I'm slingin' this shit on the table!

JUDITH: And there are other reasons. Just where I am, you know? I'm a romantic, I guess, and I assume there is something worth doing, that active is better than passive. But I feel on the edge of falling, or freezing.

LUCILLE: [*Shakes her head.*] When I was your age— *madone* ... !

JUDITH: Maybe it's harder for us, now. The war's over, no one much is ethnic anymore, there aren't many jobs. When there were marches and strikes and moratoriums, people didn't think much about the future, they were distracted, sort of a hippie bread and circuses idea.

LUCILLE: [*Nods her head, but she doesn't understand one word.*] Yeah.

JUDITH: No one had time to worry about how they'd live five years from now—it was all now. Everybody could be a hero, occupy a dean's office, publish his memoirs, have them serialized in *The New York Times*—

LUCILLE: Wit the small print!

JUDITH: And you have to wonder, all that energy, and that

courage, was it just adolescence? Sometimes I'm afraid. Just afraid. Maybe we're at the end of the spiral which people once thought endless. Maybe it's running out. I don't want it to be over. Francis is afraid too. But together ... I'm sorry, I'm not making any sense, I didn't sleep much.

LUCILLE: But you didn't buy him a birthday present.

JUDITH: Is that important?

LUCILLE: Vital. It's the gesture. Don' matter what it is but you got to make the gesture. It shows respect. It shows you're serious. No birthday present and he's gotta right to wonder if you mean it. It's like an outward sign. You just can't go around sayin', I need you, or I love you, and then ignorin' them on special occasions. That don' make no sense. So you buy them the birthday present, you send them the card, you go visit them inna hospital, you bake them the cake—you show them respect. *Cabisce?* Respect!

JUDITH: *Sì.*

LUCILLE: *Bene.* All you can do is try and hope. That's how I got my husband, may God forgive him, and may he rest in peace. You really like Francis? Come on, you come wit me to Wanamaker's we buy Francis a present we cheer ourselves up.

[FRAN *comes out of* BUNNY's *house.*]

FRAN: Yo, Lucille!

LUCILLE: Judith and me's goin' ta Wanamaker's to buy Francis a present.

FRAN: See youse later, be good and be careful.

[LUCILLE *and* JUDITH *exit through the gate.* FRANCIS *comes racing out of* BUNNY's *house.*]

FRAN: Yo, where you goin'?

FRANCIS: Nowhere.

FRAN: You got company.

FRANCIS: I didn't invite them.

FRAN: [*Embraces* FRANCIS.] Happy birthday, son.

FRANCIS: Don't hang on me so much.

FRAN: What are you afraid of? You got somewhere to go you take some coin. [*Offers him some money.*]

FRANCIS: I don't need any money.

FRAN: Well, take some more.

FRANCIS: I don't need any more.

FRAN: Take!

FRANCIS: I don't need it!!

FRAN: Look, my son, I'm gonna give you a piece of advice I learned from the army, from dealin' wit your mother, and from twenty years in the printers' union: Take! Take wit both hands, both feet, and your mouth too. If your ass is flexible enough take wit that, use your knees and your elbows, train your balls and take! *Prend'— cabisce?* Somebody offers you somethin', you take it, then run . . . [*Puts the money in* FRANCIS's *shirt pocket.*] . . . but always say thank you first. And look, if there's ever anything, well, that conventional people, not like us Geminiani Italians—but other people might be ashamed of, don't ever be afraid to come to me, no matter how hard it is, I'll understand—understand?

FRANCIS: I don't understand. [*Suddenly embraces his father.*] But I understand, okay? [*Runs out through the gate.*]

FRAN: Where you goin'?

FRANCIS: To buy some diet soda.

FRAN: That diet crap is gonna kill ya.

[RANDY *comes out of* BUNNY's *house, trailed by* HER-SCHEL.]

RANDY: Where's Francis?

FRAN: He went to buy diet crap.

HERSCHEL: [*Grabs* RANDY's *arm and starts pulling him toward the alley.*] Maybe we'll pass him, you know, like on our way to the trolleys. . . .

RANDY: [*Freeing himself*] Is there a pool around here? I'd like to go swimming.

FRAN: Yeah.

HERSCHEL: You promised!

FRAN: There's a community center about four blocks from here, Herschel can go with you. You can change here.

RANDY: Great.

[RANDY *crawls into the tent to change.* BUNNY *comes out of her house, eating a sandwich.*]

BUNNY: Hey, Herschel, I thought you was draggin' Beau Brummel to the trolleys—

HERSCHEL: He wants to go swimming.

BUNNY: Why don't you go wit him?

HERSCHEL: [*Under his breath*] Fuck!

BUNNY: Where's the birthday boy?

FRAN: He took off.

BUNNY: Helluva way to treat company. Prob'ly went to buy a opera record.

RANDY: [*Still inside the tent*] He already has thousands.

FRAN: [*To* BUNNY] Look, I got stuff to do, gotta buy Francis a birthday cake. Bun, you wanna come?

BUNNY: Sure, I could use a doughnut or two.

[*They exit through the gate.* HERSCHEL *picks up his tricycle.*]

HERSCHEL: Randy, Randy!

RANDY: [*From inside the tent*] What?

HERSCHEL: Would you like to play trolley?

RANDY: How?

HERSCHEL: Just call ding, when I ask you to. Like . . . [*Pipes out.*] Ding!

RANDY: Okay.

HERSCHEL: [*Careening around the yard like a trolley, making a lot of noise*] Ritner! . . . Now.

RANDY: Ding!

HERSCHEL: Good. [*Careens.*] Tasker! . . . Now.

RANDY: Ding!

HERSCHEL: Dickinson! . . . Now. [*Silence.*] Now. Oh, you missed that one.

RANDY: [*Comes out of the tent, in a T-shirt and shorts.*] Ding!

[HERSCHEL *is gaping at him.*]

RANDY: Do you think I look weird?

[HERSCHEL *shakes his head "no."*]

RANDY: I mean, skinny.

HERSCHEL: I think you look, like, you know—

RANDY: Yeah, yeah. But do you think my legs are too thin?

HERSCHEL: Oh no!

RANDY: Boy, it's rough being this thin, you know, I've tried to put on at least ten pounds. I bought two quarts of this stuff called Wate-On.

HERSCHEL: [*Points to his stomach.*] Oh yeah, like "weight on"—

RANDY: Putrid stuff. I drank a quart of it, tastes like milk of magnesia, I got sick for a week and lost ten pounds.

HERSCHEL: I tried to kill myself by drinking a quart of milk of magnesia once; but I didn't lose any weight.

[FRANCIS *enters through the gate, drinking a diet soda. A tense moment between* FRANCIS *and* RANDY.]

RANDY: We're going swimming.

FRANCIS: I'll stay here.

RANDY: Okay, Herschel, let's go. . . .

[*They start off; suddenly* RANDY *staggers, clutches the air, twists about, acts dizzy, and falls to the ground. He is faking a petit mal.*]

HERSCHEL: [*Very alarmed*] Randy, what is it?

FRANCIS: [*Catching on*] Looks like a petit mal, Herschel.

HERSCHEL: No, no, that's epilepsy. Take your belt off!

FRANCIS: Why?

HERSCHEL: So he won't bite his tongue off. Give it to me! [*Sticks belt in* RANDY'S *mouth.*] I'll go get my medicine! [*Rushes into his house.*]

RANDY: [*Who has been writhing on the ground until now, suddenly sits up.*] Are you a faggot?

[HERSCHEL *comes running out with a bottle of medicine.* RANDY *starts writhing again.*]

HERSCHEL: Here—you have to shake it first!

FRANCIS: [*Shaking the bottle*] I think he'll need some Valium too—

HERSCHEL: Good idea! [*Runs into house and reappears almost instantly.*] Fives or tens?

FRANCIS: Fives should do it.

[HERSCHEL *races into house.*]

RANDY: [*Sits up, dropping the fit.*] I mean homosexual— I mean, gay person—

HERSCHEL: [*Racing back out*] We're out!

[RANDY *fakes the fit again.*]

FRANCIS: Do you have any aspirin?

RANDY: [*Mumbling unintelligibly*] Aspirin upsets my stomach!

FRANCIS: Aspirin upsets his stomach.

HERSCHEL: Tylenol?

FRANCIS: Tylenol?

RANDY: Tylenol!

HERSCHEL and FRANCIS: Tylenol!

HERSCHEL: I'll go get some! [*Races off through the alley.*]

RANDY: [*He stands, dusts himself off, awkward pause.*] When we talked and all that, you know in your room, were you just trying to make me?

FRANCIS: I don't know.

RANDY: I don't care that much, but it's worse being treated like you were laying a trap for me. And I didn't think you were gay—odd maybe. Have there . . . [*He realizes how silly this is going to sound.*] . . . been many before me?

FRANCIS: Well, starting in high school, there was Max. He was a poet, a Libra, on the fencing team, short and dark, compact you might say, very dashing with his épées. Then there were George and Eliot, they were twins. Then, Sheldon Gold, briefly.

RANDY: How many did you sleep with?

FRANCIS: Sleep with? They didn't even talk to me.

RANDY: You never told them how you felt?

FRANCIS: Well, that's it, you see. I'm never sure how I feel, really.

RANDY: Have you ever had sex with a man?

[FRANCIS *shakes his head "no."*]

RANDY: Were there girls before Judith?

FRANCIS: Well, there was Elaine Hoffenburg. She had braces.

RANDY: Braces on her teeth?

FRANCIS: Legs. I took her to the senior prom. [RANDY *looks incredulous.*] Well, I was no catch, either. I was very fat then. It wasn't too bad. Once she got enough momentum going, she could do a passable waltz. Then there was Luise Morely. Slightly pockmarked but pretty in a plain sort of way. We held hands through *The Sandpiper,* then we did it afterward. It was my first time. Elaine had been willing, but it was a little hard getting her legs apart.

RANDY: Gross! I worked for months to get Nancy Simmons to go to the prom with me, then I got car-sick on the way and threw up all over her; and you remember Roberta Hasserfluth, I broke up with her just as you and Judith got together, well, we decided we would do it, so we went to the drive-in movie in Waltham. It was *The Four Stewardesses—*

FRANCIS: Wasn't that in 3-D?

RANDY: Oh, was it ever, we had to wear goggles and everything. Well, I bought this bottle of Mateus, see, and since I'd never bought wine before I forgot you needed a corkscrew. So I couldn't get it open, so there we are watching this dirty movie in the dead of winter, with this bottle of Mateus between my legs, trying to get it open with my car key—

FRANCIS: Well, did you ever do it?

RANDY: Too cold! I'm sort of a jerk with girls, but I like them. I like you too, you're my friend. But I don't think I'm in love with you. Does that mean you were in love with me? [FRANCIS *shrugs.*] I mean, Francis, has it ever occurred to you you might be suffering from homosexual panic?

FRANCIS: [*Snaps his fingers.*] I knew I should have taken Psych. 101.

'RANDY: I mean, it's true. It's really common in a competitive society. My father was suffering from homosexual panic last year. He took his secretary Betsy to Europe to cure it. He got in trouble with the IRS over it. He said anything that cures him of homosexuality ought to be deductible.

FRANCIS: [*Shakes his head, irritated at being put on.*] Oh, really.

RANDY: I'm serious. I mean, if you've never slept with a man, never laid a hand on me . . .

FRANCIS: Are you saying that if you were to strip right now and lie down inside that tent, I couldn't—well, do anything?

RANDY: Well, there's only one way to find out. [*Starts to strip.*]

FRANCIS: What are you doing? Randy, what are you doing?

RANDY: I'm stripping.

FRANCIS: Are you crazy? In front of me? Here?
[FRANCIS *makes a dash for his door, but* RANDY *intercepts him.* RANDY *stands in front of the door, blocking it. He looks around the yard, up at the windows, then unzips his fly.*]

FRANCIS: Jesus Christ!

RANDY: [*Walks over to the tent.*] I'll save the rest for inside the tent. [*Crawls inside.*] [*Peeks out*] When you think of this, and you will, be kind! [*Disappears*]

FRANCIS: Randy! [*Anxious*] Randy? Jesus Christ! Oh, Jesus—

FRANCIS: Jesus Christ! Oh, Jesus . . . [*Holding his chin*] I didn't shave this morning.

[FRANCIS *is about to crawl into the tent as* HERSCHEL *comes bounding in from the alley.*]

HERSCHEL: How's Randy?

FRANCIS: [*Exasperated*] Jesus Christ, Herschel, he's dead!

HERSCHEL: [*Horror-struck*] He is??!!

FRANCIS: Ten minutes ago; heart failure.

HERSCHEL: Are you sure? I mean, I faked a heart attack in gym class last month. Maybe he's faking. Call an ambulance!

FRANCIS: Damn it, Herschel, he's dead, now go away!

HERSCHEL: Can I see the body?

RANDY: [*Sticks his head out of the tent.*] Hello, Herschel.

HERSCHEL: Randy! He said . . .

RANDY: I heard. Look, Herschel, Francis and I—

FRANCIS: [*Trying to stop him*] Randy!

RANDY: —are involved in a very serious ritual. We will both be drummed out of our exclusive clubs at Harvard if we don't do this.

HERSCHEL: Oh, heavy.

RANDY: Very. So, Herschel, would you please go away and come back a little later?

HERSCHEL: Sure.

[*He sets a little bottle of Tylenol in front of the tent and starts for the alley.* RANDY *throws the shorts out at* FRANCIS. HERSCHEL *turns back.*]

HERSCHEL: Like five minutes?

FRANCIS: [*Grabs the shorts, hides them behind his back.*] Herschel, take a long walk!

[HERSCHEL, *dejected, exits out the alley.* FRANCIS *hesitates, peers into the tent, and finally crawls inside. There is no movement for a few seconds, then* RANDY, *wrapped in the sleeping bag, comes bounding out of the tent, followed by* FRANCIS.]

FRANCIS: Randy, what's the matter? What's the matter? Why did you strip if you didn't mean it? Were you bringing me on?

RANDY: No! [*Runs back into the tent.*]

FRANCIS: Is that what was going on this spring? Perhaps somewhere in some subconscious avenue of that boyman mind of yours you sensed I had a vulnerable point and decided to make the most of it?

RANDY: [*From inside the tent*] I was seventeen fucking years old this spring—what's your excuse?

FRANCIS: Well, you're eighteen now.

RANDY: [*Coming out of tent, wearing jeans*] I liked you!

FRANCIS: [*Sarcastic*] Thanks!

RANDY: I really did.

FRANCIS: It's vicious of you.

RANDY: How?

FRANCIS: Because you did it all just to humiliate me—

RANDY: I really do like you. I mean, liking does exist, doesn't it? It doesn't have to include sex, or love, or deep need, does it?

FRANCIS: I don't know.

RANDY: I don't know either.

FRANCIS: I don't know either.

RANDY: Boy . . . you are really fucked up. [*He embraces* FRANCIS.]

FRANCIS: I know.

[*He puts his arms around* RANDY. JUDITH *enters the yard from the gate carrying a large gaily wrapped box. She sees this embrace and lets out a surprised yell. The two jump apart, confused, and looking guilty.*]

RANDY: Judith!

JUDITH: You're disgusting!

RANDY: It's not my fault, he's older than I am!

JUDITH: He's younger than you are!

FRANCIS: Judith . . .

JUDITH: [*Turns on him.*] And you!

FRANCIS: Now, look, Judith, it didn't have anything to do with sex!

JUDITH: Oh no! I'm sure! Nothing you do has anything to do with sex! It's all a bring-on, isn't it? You get to that point, and then you're ugly, or you're fat, or you're gay! What did you use on him? That you were ugly, fat, and straight? Well, I'm on to you! Happy birthday! [*She throws the box at* FRANCIS.]

FRANCIS: Act your age, Judith!

JUDITH: Oh ho, act my age, act my age says this paragon of maturity, this pristine sage now come of age!

FRANCIS: It's hard to explain. . . .

RANDY: That's right!

JUDITH: Hard? Hard to explain? What is? You're going to fuck my brother, that's very simple, that's the birds and the bees, that's Biology 1A. I thought I loved you. I thought I loved you! [*Starts hitting* RANDY.] I thought I loved him!

FRANCIS: Judith, will you please calm down.

JUDITH: And my mother told me never to trust fatties, they're self-indulgent. Go have a banana split!

RANDY: For Christ' sake, calm down!

JUDITH: I knew there was something suspicious in your wanting to come along. I bet the two of you were laughing at me, comparing notes, carrying on behind my back the whole time. Why, Francis, why would you do this to me?

FRANCIS: He was bringing me on, standing here with no clothes on, hanging on to me, what would you do?

JUDITH: Puke!

RANDY: Do you think I enjoyed it? Huh, tubby?

JUDITH: [*To* RANDY] So you're a faggot too—won't the sophomore class be surprised?

RANDY: Why are you screaming at me, it's his fault!

FRANCIS: [*Shaking his finger at* RANDY] It's your fault!

JUDITH: Oh, my God, it's love! M and M—mutual masturbation!

RANDY: [*Angry*] I thought I could help him, I should have known better, I can't help you—
[*Shoves* FRANCIS. HERSCHEL *comes bounding in from alley.*]

HERSCHEL: Randy, your ceremony seems to be over, we can go see the . . .

RANDY: [*Screaming, runs into tent.*] And I can't help you either, Herschel!

HERSCHEL: Francis . . .

FRANCIS: God damn it, Herschel, go away!

HERSCHEL: Oh, no, I did it again!
[JUDITH *is on one side of the stage, talking to* FRANCIS, *and* HERSCHEL *is on the other side, talking to the tent.*]

JUDITH: And I was even out buying you a present!

HERSCHEL: I tried to be your friend, I don't know how . . .

JUDITH: And I was willing to be understanding.

HERSCHEL: I'm just stupid.

JUDITH: All those Callas records, and I hate her voice and her wobble!

FRANCIS: She only wobbles on the late recordings!

HERSCHEL: What did I do?

JUDITH: And that "Toti dal Monte," for Christ' sake, she sounds like a broken steam engine!

FRANCIS: Her mad scene is still the best on records!

HERSCHEL: It's just me!

JUDITH: And what about my mad scene?

HERSCHEL: I'm just retarded like they all say! [*He runs into his house.*]

RANDY: [*From inside the tent*] Shut up, Judith!

JUDITH: Oh, God, and I even came here bringing your beloved! And you kissed me, and you stroked me, and we held hands along the Charles River, and I thought: He's weird, he's pudgy, he likes Maria Callas, but he responds to me! What a laugh! That's funnier than *The Barber of Seville*, that's funnier than *The Girl of the Golden West*—

FRANCIS: Shut up, shut up, Judith, God damn it, act your age! You're like a fucking six-year-old!

JUDITH: And you? How old are you?!

[*They are right in front of the Geminiani door.* BUNNY, FRAN, *and* LUCILLE *enter grandly from* FRAN's *house, carrying a huge birthday cake and singing. They are wearing party hats.* BUNNY *is running around, putting hats on* JUDITH *and* FRANCIS, *and* RANDY, *as he emerges from the tent.* FRAN *has the cake on the same typing table that was used for breakfast. He also has a camera.*]

BUNNY, FRAN, *and* LUCILLE:
    Happy birthday to you,
    Happy birthday to you,
    Happy birthday, dear Francis,
    Happy birthday to you!

FRAN: Happy birthday, my son! [*Snaps a picture.*]

LUCILLE: Come on, blow out the candles and cut the cake, it's too hot to wait.

BUNNY: There's only six candles, all we could find.

[FRANCIS *is about to blow them out.*]

LUCILLE: Come on, make a wish.

[*He does.* FRAN *takes another picture, and* FRANCIS *blows out the candles. They all cheer and applaud.* JUDITH *and* RANDY *are still stunned.*]

FRANCIS: Thank you. I would first like to thank my father, now that I am officially an adult, for teaching me how to dance and sing and cough and fart and scratch and above all how to treat a rash once it becomes visible to the general public, then I would like to thank my next-door neighbor Bunny . . .

[FRAN *snaps a photo of* BUNNY.]

FRANCIS: . . . for demonstrating once and for all that motherhood ought to be abolished, along with drunks and whores; Lucille, for teaching me how to ruin the happiest occasion with one glance and the cheapest insect spray; and Randy, for providing us with living proof of the vacuity of American Higher Education; and then Judith, our brilliant, bubbly, and, let's not forget, mature Italian major from Radcliffe will recite to us in her Main Line Italian all the nonsense syllables of her upbringing and her recent reading. And I want you all to know precisely what I think of all this: this neighborhood, Bunny and Lucille, Randy and Judith!

[*He rips into the cake with his hands and tears it apart, hurling pieces at* JUDITH *and the others. All duck away. After* FRANCIS *has destroyed the cake, he runs off through the gate.* HERSCHEL *stumbles out of his house, holding the bag of rat poison, powder all over his mouth.*]

HERSCHEL: I swallowed Uncle Eddie's rat poison!

BUNNY: My baby!

FRAN: Holy shit!

BUNNY: [*On her knees by* HERSCHEL] My baby!

LUCILLE: Who's gonna clean it up, hanh?

BLACKOUT

Scene 2

Evening. FRAN *has a huge trash bag and is cleaning up the yard.* LUCILLE *is sitting on the divider between the two houses.* RANDY *is finishing packing. Their tent has been struck and is rolled up again.*

LUCILLE: Rum and chocolate sauce everywhere—did he know how much it cost?

FRAN: Well, it was his birthday cake, if he wanted a throw it around, it's his right I guess.

LUCILLE: But it ain't his right to clean it up, hanh? [*She points to a piece of cake.*] Over there. Jesus, I'm sick and tired of cleanin' up afta people. [*Points again.*] Over here. Cleanin' up afta my brothers . . .

FRAN: [*Under his breath, still picking up*] Your brothers . . .

LUCILLE: Afta Pop . . .

FRAN: Afta Pop . . .

LUCILLE: Then my mom got senile . . .

FRAN: Then Mom . . .

LUCILLE: Then my husband . . .

FRAN: Your husband . . .

LUCILLE: Then Donny . . .

FRAN: [*Joking*] Ain't he at Yale?

LUCILLE: Hanh? Of course he's at Yale, that's a stupid question, *ma stupidezza. . . .*

RANDY: I'll see if Judith is ready. [*Runs into* BUNNY'S *house.*]

FRAN: I hope Francis gets back soon—I think his guests are gonna leave any minute—

LUCILLE: Well, I'm surprised they stayed as long as they did. Well, at least he didn't play so much opera music this weekend—all that screamin'—that's what I got against opera, Fran, ain't like real life.
[*She tries to clean up some whipped cream with a Kleenex.* BUNNY *enters from her house, depressed.*]

BUNNY: Yo, Fran.

FRAN: Yo, Bun. How's Herschel?

BUNNY: Better and better, just ate all my leftovers.

FRAN: I guess they're gettin' ready to leave.

BUNNY: Yep.

LUCILLE: [*About* BUNNY, *mean*] *E questa si chiama una madre?*

FRAN: Lucille, take this bag in the house—tape up the top so nothin' gets in. . . .
[LUCILLE *takes the bag and goes into* FRAN'S *house. He calls after her.*]

FRAN: And put on the coffee!

BUNNY: [*Sits down on her stoop.*] She could use a enema, lye and hot pepper! [*Looks at* FRAN.] Remember way back when, when we did it?

FRAN: Oh, Bun.

BUNNY: Oh, Fran! 'Sbeen a long time. I think it's time we did it again. Don't say it, you got Lucille! What's Lucille? Shit, she gotta get on the subway to get her hips movin'.

FRAN: You don' need me, Bun.

BUNNY: We was good together.

FRAN: How often? Five times the most? I remember the first time. [*He sits down beside her.*] You remember? We forced Francis to take Herschel to the movies; it was *Lady and the Tramp*. They was that young, we could force them. Can you see the two of them together?

BUNNY: They was both so fat they probably took up a whole row between them.

FRAN: Didn't they have rashes too?

BUNNY: Nah, that was the third time. We forced Francis to take Herschel into Center City to buy calamine lotion.

[*She puts her head on his shoulder. He looks up to his window, checking for* LUCILLE.]

FRAN: Why don't you give Sam a call?

BUNNY: He ain't interested.

FRAN: I bet you still like him.

BUNNY: You still like your wife?

FRAN: Sure, I married her, didn't I? We went together two years and were pretty happy until Francis came along. She wasn't the same after that. Oh well, she's gone. And now there's Lucille—at least she bakes good fiadone. And she's good people, even if she schives too much. I mean, what kinda choice I got? Hanh? Women today, they look at you, they see a man wheezin', coughin', goin' to the bathroom, scratchin', gettin' rashes, they take off. But Sam ain't attached yet—give him a call, fix yourself up, grow up a little—

BUNNY: Grow up a little? Like that was easy. Jesus, if only I didn't still act and feel nineteen. I look in the mirror and I know there's fat and wrinkles there, Jesus Christ do I know there's fat and wrinkles! Yet I'll be damned if I don't still, somewhere in there, see this nineteen-year-old filly hot to trot and on fire for some kind of success in life! [*Looks at house, tricycle.*] And look what I got—

FRAN: So Herschel's a little crazy, but he's gonna do wonders—

BUNNY: He's a fuckin' genius! Grow up a little. And what about Francis?

FRAN: Don' know, this Judith girl—

BUNNY: She seems to like him, hard as that is to believe, but I don't see much evidence of his liking her.

FRAN: No, I guess not, but kids nowadays, maybe they act different when they're goin' together—and maybe she isn't his last chance.

BUNNY: Don't kid yourself. Look, why don't you just ask him and save yourself years of wonderin' and never bein' sure . . . ?

FRAN: It's the hardest thing for a father to ask his son. Don' know why it should be, I know guys who . . . like . . . other guys who are regular, you know, in every other way. But you know, it's his life now, he's gonna pay the consequences for whatever he does . . . but still, I hope.

BUNNY: Well, I worry about Herschel too. But Jesus, I figure we're lucky if he lives to be twenty-one—

LUCILLE: [*Appears in the doorway.*] Yo, Fran!

FRAN: [*Gets away from* BUNNY.] Yo, Lucille!

LUCILLE: I see the monster comin' down the street—[*She goes back in.*]

FRAN: Bunny, let's go inside, he won't want to see us right off—

[*They go into* BUNNY's *house.* FRANCIS *enters from the gate. He sees the packed knapsacks under the fig tree. After a moment,* JUDITH *enters from* BUNNY's *house. She is wearing a skirt and blouse.*]

JUDITH: Well . . . Azazel has returned.

FRANCIS: Who?

JUDITH: Who else? The Prodigal!

[LUCILLE *comes out of* FRAN's *house, carrying a coffee pot and a new robe for* HERSCHEL. *She sees* FRANCIS.]

LUCILLE: *Ma Sporcaccione!* [*She slams the door, and goes into* BUNNY's *house.*]

FRANCIS: Is everyone furious at me?

JUDITH: We have Bunny's uncle on the force waiting inside with handcuffs.

FRANCIS: Oh, Jesus, you're at it again—

JUDITH: Well, to be serious, Lucille is making a novena

to Saint Jude the Obscure, Patron Saint of the Hopeless and Pudgy who spoil their own birthday parties. [*She gets a sweater out of her knapsack.*] Herschel took rat poison.

FRANCIS: Is he dead?

JUDITH: No more than ever. Bunny called her uncle on the ambulance squad and he was rushed to St. Agnes Hospital, across Track Thirty-seven on the A, the AA one through seven, and the B express lines, perhaps you've passed it? They cleaned up the yard as best they could, but you'll probably be finding birthday cake here and there for the next few months. Still, the fall rains and the march of time should wash away all stains from your yard, your life, and these, the Days of our Youth! Thank you.

FRANCIS: And you're leaving.

JUDITH: You noticed! Maybe you aren't autistic. Yes, we're walking over to Broad Street, where we will get a cab to Thirtieth Street Station, where we will take the nine oh five train to Boston, from there we're going to our summer home. We are not hitching, you'll notice, we've lost the stomach for it. Oh, by the way, happy birthday.

FRANCIS: Thank you.

JUDITH: I'm sorry.

FRANCIS: So am I.

[*They are about to go to each other, when* RANDY *comes out of* BUNNY's *house.*]

RANDY: C'mon, Judith. We have nineteen minutes to catch that train.

[FRAN *and* LUCILLE *come out of* BUNNY's *house.*]

FRAN: So, Igor's back, hanh? I guess you kids is off.

[RANDY *and* JUDITH *are putting on their knapsacks and collecting their belongings.*]

RANDY: We're off!

LUCILLE: Good-bye!

FRAN: The way I see it, life is made up of hellos and good-byes and forgivin' and forgettin'. So you two forgive and forget and come back, hanh? Even if Frankenstein ain't here, you're always welcome.

[BUNNY *comes out of her house with* HERSCHEL. *He is wearing clean pajamas and a new bathrobe.*]

BUNNY: [*Sees* FRANCIS.] So, Igor's back, hanh? [*To* RANDY

and JUDITH] We wanted to see youse off, you're good
people, you kids.

LUCILLE: [*To* JUDITH] If I give you Donny's number at
Yale, maybe you could get in touch with him this fall,
he's nice, real good-looking, and athletic, and he ain't
no party pooper neither. [*She gives* JUDITH *a slip of
paper.*] I have somethin' in the house for you. [*She goes
inside.*]

HERSCHEL: [*To* RANDY, *shyly*] Like, if I promise to lose
weight and get less weird, can we be friends?

RANDY: Sure, even if you gain and get weirder.

HERSCHEL: Like, don't lie to me, you know? Like, I understand if you aren't interested. But can I, like, you
know, write you letters?

RANDY: Oh sure. I'll give you our summer address, otherwise, just write me at Harvard.

[*He writes address on a little piece of paper that*
HERSCHEL *had ready.* LUCILLE *returns with a plate
wrapped in tin foil. The following three lines are said
at about the same time.*]

JUDITH: C'mon, Randy, let's go!

LUCILLE: C'mon, Randy, you're gonna miss the train.

RANDY: See you, Herschel.

[JUDITH, FRAN, *and* LUCILLE *go out through the gate.
They stand in the entrance saying final good-byes.*
RANDY, *about to say good-bye to Francis, is grabbed
by* BUNNY.]

BUNNY: Oh, honey bun, I feel like I've known you for
years. Maybe I'm gettin' funny in the head, but I know
a promising hunk when I see one.

RANDY: Thank you.

BUNNY: I'm gonna miss you.

[RANDY *smiles and tries to get away, but she hangs
on.*]

JUDITH: [*Calling from the gate*] C'mon, Randy!

BUNNY: Be careful when you sit down on toilets, put paper there, you hear? And see that some people may be
pretty, even if they got strange faces, and mean well,
even if they act weird, and think of me once in a while,
hanh? [*She kisses him.*] Goodbye!

[*She goes into her house.* HERSCHEL *and* RANDY *shake
hands, then* HERSCHEL, *looking back sadly, blinking
back tears, follows his mother into the house.*]

RANDY: [*Goes to* FRANCIS.] In the fall, right?

FRANCIS: Right.

[*They shake hands.*]

JUDITH: Randy!

RANDY: Listen, I was just trying to help, okay?

[RANDY *leaves. The good-byes are heard from behind the fence.* FRANCIS *is left alone.*]

FRAN: Come back soon! Please!

[FRANCIS *goes into his room and puts on a quiet, sad piece of music.* FRAN *and* LUCILLE *come back into the yard.*]

FRAN: Let's go to your place, hanh? Need some coffee.

LUCILLE: I got some nice cheesecake for you, Fran.

FRAN: Yeah? Sounds good. [*Yells to* FRANCIS.] Yo, Francis! We're goin' a Lucille's for coffee and cake. Wanna come? [*There is no answer.*] Yo, Francis!

FRANCIS: [*From his room*] God damn it, no!

FRAN: That's my Ivy League son.

[FRAN *and* LUCILLE *exit through the gate.* FRANCIS *appears in his window. He is very agitated. The music is playing.*]

FRANCIS: Jesus Christ, what am I doing? [*Calls out.*] Dad! Dad! Yo, Dad! [*He runs out of the house to the gate.*]

FRAN: [*Heard from offstage*] What is it?

FRANCIS: Give me some coin, I'm going to Boston! [*Runs back into his room.*]

FRAN: [*Running into yard*] Jesus Christ in heaven! Yo, Bun!

[BUNNY'S *lights go on.* FRANCIS *turns off the music.*]

BUNNY: [*At her window*] Yo, Fran!

FRAN: Call your uncle on the ambulance service. We gotta get Francis to the train!

BUNNY: Holy shit! [*She goes to her telephone in the kitchen.*]

LUCILLE: [*Running into house*] I'll help you pack.

BUNNY: [*On the phone*] Hello, Uncle Marty, bring your fuckin' ambulance down, we gotta make a train!

HERSCHEL: [*Coming out of his house*] What's going on?

FRAN: Francis is going to Boston.

HERSCHEL: To see Randy?

BUNNY: [*Still on the phone*] Hello, Uncle Jimmy, send a fuckin' squad car down, we gotta make a train.

FRAN: Hey, Herschel! Catch them kids. [*Pushes him to the gate.*]

HERSCHEL: This way's quicker! [*Runs out through alley behind his house.*]

FRAN: [*Yelling after him*] And bring them back! I'm fuckin' outa money. Lucille!

LUCILLE: [*In* FRANCIS's *room, with a large laundry bag*] There ain't no clean clothes in here!

FRAN: You got some money? I'm out.

LUCILLE: [*Hurling coin purse out the window*] Look!

FRANCIS: Oh, I want to take my new records—Callas in *Parsifal*, 1950, and the 1955 *Norma*! [*Runs into his room.*]

FRAN: [*Going through change purse*] Jesus Christ, Lucille, all these pennies!

LUCILLE: For the tax!

FRAN: Yo, Bun!

BUNNY: Yo, Fran!

FRAN: We need some more money!

[BUNNY *comes out of her house, reaches into her bosom, and removes wad.*]

BUNNY: Here's the house money, take what you need. [*Sirens are heard in the distance, getting closer.*] They're comin'!

[FRANCIS *runs out of the house, holding record albums.*]

BUNNY: You stick wit me, kid, I got connections! [*Hugs* FRANCIS, *as* FRAN *counts money.*] Where's Gargantua!

FRAN: He went to get the kids. [*To* FRANCIS] I think this is enough— [*Gives him money.*]

BUNNY: I hope he doesn't frighten them away!

LUCILLE: [*Runs out of the house with the laundry bag.*] This is the best I could do—go to a laundromat when you get there!

FRANCIS: [*Takes bag, hugs her.*] Thanks everybody, I mean, thanks. . . .

FRAN: Well, it's your birthday.

[*Sirens increase.* HERSCHEL *comes running in from the alley with* JUDITH *and* RANDY.]

HERSCHEL: I got 'em! I got 'em!

FRAN: They're back!

[FRANCIS *embraces* JUDITH. *Sirens much louder.*]

BUNNY: [*At gate.*] My uncles is here!
[*The kids run out. The others watch at the gate.*]
FRAN: [*Checks his watch, then puts his arms around* LUCILLE *and* BUNNY.] I think they're gonna make it!

BLACKOUT

The Transfiguration of Benno Blimpie

The stage is divided as follows:

BENNO'S ROOM

BENNO, an enormously fat young man of twenty, sits on a stool from which he can survey the action comfortably. This is in an area somewhat removed from the rest of the stage. The area represents BENNO's current room, in which he has barricaded himself. He sits on his stool for the entire length of the play.

When BENNO is involved in a scene he acts as if he were present, and the others act the same. In these scenes he is playing a young boy, and he makes this plain by changing his voice slightly so that it is higher.

His clothes are very large on him, and tentlike. They look as if they haven't been washed or changed in weeks. His complexion is blotchy and pockmarked. His hair is greasy and full of tangles.

THE PARK

This is another area, where trash and dead leaves are scattered about. It is inhabited by the GIRL and the OLD MAN—all their scenes take place here.

The OLD MAN is BENNO's grandfather, an Italian immigrant, about seventy. The GIRL is from the neighborhood, thirteen, tough, Irish parents.

THE KITCHEN

A third area, this represents the kitchen in the home of

BENNO'S PARENTS, and of the young BENNO. Once again, this is an area somewhat isolated, and it should reflect an urban working-class home.

Benno's parents are seen as they were when he was a young boy. His father is in his early thirties or very late twenties, good-looking, a former athlete. His mother is older than the father, less attractive.

It should be kept in mind that Benno is remembering the scenes that are acted out on stage. Thus he is controlling them. He watches these scenes with great intensity and concentration.

Scene 1

Lights up on BENNO, *eating.*

In dim light, one by one, MOTHER, FATHER, GIRL, OLD
MAN *in characteristic poses.*

They freeze. BENNO *finishes eating and speaks to the
audience.*

BENNO: I am Benno. I am eating myself to death.

BLACKOUT

Scene 2

Lights up on Benno. He speaks to the audience.

BENNO: And there were weeds, feet, and bugs. There
were black ants and red ants and giant ants and worms.
There were worms and spiders and snails. One day I
crushed one hundred eighteen snails with my bare feet.
I was very fat even then. It was after a rainstorm. I ran
in the grass and took off my shoes and socks. The snails
inched out and I smashed every one I saw for an hour.
I had snail blood all over my feet. My grandfather asked
me what it was.
OLD MAN: [*The Park. He speaks as though* BENNO *were
a little boy standing beside him.*] Eh, Benno, what you
got all over your feet, hanh? You mother gonna give me

hell. Why can't you look afta yourself, hanh? What is that shit on you feet?

BENNO: [*High voice, playing little boy, acting as though he were beside the* OLD MAN] Snail wine.

OLD MAN: You crazy, crazy!

[*Hits where* BENNO *would be standing.* BENNO *reacts to the blow in place. The lights go down on the* OLD MAN, *but ·stay up on* BENNO. *Ice cream truck jingle heard.*]

BENNO: I have eaten seventeen chocolate cones today. Soft ice cream, the kind they sell in trucks. Those trucks announce themselves with tinkling, mechanical tunes played over and over. I heard the neighborhood truck making its rounds and I ran out and bought seventeen cones. Chocolate. I was out of breath from running down the stairs.

[*A light up on* BENNO's MOTHER *in Kitchen.* BENNO *changes his voice to a high whine.* MOTHER *reacts as though he were beside her and busies herself in the Kitchen.*]

BENNO: [*high voice*] Momma, I wanna chocolate cone.

MOTHER: You're too fat ·as it is, Benno.

BENNO: I'm hungry. I wanna chocolate cone.

MOTHER: Shut up, fatsy. Why are you so fat? Tell me that. Hanh? Why are you so fat? Well, at least fat men got big ones.

BENNO: Ma, I want one.

MOTHER: I remember old Joey Fercanti around the corner in the old neighborhood. We was growin' up together. He was fatter even than you. He took my sister and me inna the alley one day and took it out and stuffed it inna his shirt pocket. He said: God provides for fat guys. An' I turned him down. I hadda go out an' marry that father of yours, the bastid. Joey was a looker even if he was fat. Better than you, God knows. Not all them blotches in the face and he didn't fall down every ten minutes. Well . . . maybe God'll give you a big one, but sure as hell, I doubt it.

BENNO: Ma, please, I want one.

MOTHER: Shut your face, fat jerk!

[*Lights dim out on* MOTHER.]

BENNO: [*To audience*] Mother. I used to think my father dropped roaches down her slit and that's why I heard her high giggle at night. There was no door between their room and mine; just a curtain with a rip in it. I heard her high giggle and I thought my father must have collected a lot of cockroaches that night in the cellar and was dropping them down her drain. A lot of them twisting in her tubes; suffocating, fornicating, giving birth; you know, whatever cockroaches do in cunts. And when she went into the bathroom and washed afterward, you see, I thought she was flooding them out and down the toilet. Then one night I watched through the rip in the curtain. I preferred the cockroaches. Father.

[FATHER *enters tossing a football.*]

FATHER: And now, playing center quarterback and primary receiver for Bishop Neumann, Number 64, Dominick Vertucci! [*He plays wildly, pantomiming a frenzied football game. He plays as though he were the star of the team and is driving them to victory. He pantomimes hearing cheers for himself and raises his hands over his head in victory.*] Geez, geez, thanks, I couldna done it without the guys—thanks, geez. . . . [*Catches himself, becomes flustered and shamefaced.*] Aw, shit, was only pretendin', Benno. Even I pretend sometimes. Gotta go home anyways. You bitch mother raise hell if we're late. Come on, Benno. [*Leaves sadly. As though taking* BENNO's *hand*] Don't trip over this curb. . . .

[BENNO *trips.*]

FATHER: Aw shit, Benno!

[FATHER *exits. Lights come up on the Park. The* GIRL *plays. Out of the corner of her eye she watches the* OLD MAN, *who watches her intently. She allows her game to take her close to him.*]

GIRL: [*To the* OLD MAN] Hey you! Buy me a chocolate cone.

OLD MAN: You mother, what she say?

GIRL: Who's gonna tell her?

[*A pause. She plays her game again.*]

OLD MAN: I seen you. I seen you playin' in the street. You tough. How old?

GIRL: Buy me a cone.

OLD MAN: Can't. My Social Security check ain't come this month. Down to my last dime.

GIRL: The man'll trust you. C'mon. Buy me a chocolate cone.

[*A pause.*]

OLD MAN: Come on. Benno, come on.

[*They walk off hand in hand.*]

BENNO: I was in an oven. A fat roast burning in the oven. There was a glass door to my oven and they came to it and laughed and pointed. Fat roasts are funny burning in ovens. I couldn't move. If I moved, I burned my back. If I moved, I burned my side. If I turned, old burns were given to the heat. I was trapped, you see. Once I thought, wait until you're older, Benno, wait until you're older. Strength then, and force enough to burst through the oven door into the sun, into freedom. One day I did break through the glass door. But on the other side all there was was another oven with another glass door and laughing people pointing at me. And there was no sun. Has there even been a sun? I am still in the oven, I am still in the oven, I am still in the oven. And I am burning up, trapped and pierced, burning up! That's why I am eating myself to death.

BLACKOUT

Scene 3

Lights up on the Park and on BENNO. BENNO *has a flashlight with which he plays for a moment before the scene begins.*

The Park is lit to suggest a very shady area. The light fades into heavy darkness.

The GIRL *enters barefoot. She walks slowly through the mud, humming to herself, occasionally she stops and wanders a step or two backwards.*

Very slowly, the OLD MAN *enters. He is obviously following her, and has been. The* GIRL *realizes this but doesn't show it. As she approaches the dark area she stops and plays in place. He watches her, rapt for a moment, then decides to speak.*

BENNO *pays intense attention to the scene.*

OLD MAN: What you doin' playin' inna mud?
GIRL: Walkin' barefoot.
OLD MAN: Dummy, you cut you feet.
GIRL: I want it.
OLD MAN: There are snakes and rats in here. They eat little girls, startin' down there. And swallow them, whole. Be careful.
GIRL: Ain't a little girl. An' I want to.
OLD MAN: You wanna cut you feet?
GIRL: I dunno. [*A pause. She walks a bit toward the dark area.*] Maybe a man'll come by and pick the glass outa the cut. Maybe a man'll hold my foot and lick it and cry over it.
OLD MAN: You're crazy! [*A pause.*] Men hide around here. Under them heavy trees. They hide, you hear? And they wait. For little girls to come by, barefoot. Little girls don't fight hard. [*A pause.*] Little girls, they got soft feet. Men wait with rope, to tie them, hard. Be careful!
GIRL: [*After a moment*] Take your shoes and socks off.
OLD MAN: What? Why?
GIRL: I want it. C'mon. Walk with me. Over here, in the shade, under these trees.
[*She walks into the dark area and vanishes. The* OLD MAN *waits an instant, then takes his shoes and socks off. The socks are white with a pronounced yellow tinge. He walks in after the* GIRL. BENNO *has watched and listened to this scene intently. The light brightens on him. He shines his flashlight around the area the* OLD MAN *and* GIRL *have just left—the area which isn't dark. Then shines the flashlight into his own eyes. He squints and shudders.*]
BENNO: [*Quickly, passionately*] Cimabue, Giotto, Donatello, Pico della Mirandola, Bellini, Michelangelo, Rafaello, Botticelli, Brunelleschi, I want, I want, want, want, want, Brunelleschi, Botticelli, Raffaello, Michelangelo, Bellini, Pico della Mirandola, Donatello, Giotto, Cimabue. I want, please, please, I want—wantwant-

wantwantwantwant! Give me ... give me ... [*He is panting, his eyes are shut tightly. He has begun to cry.*] No one, no one, no one ... no ... one ...
[*He shines the flashlight slowly into the dark area. The* OLD MAN *is caressing and kissing the* GIRL'*s feet. She moans. Hold a moment.*]

BLACKOUT

Scene 4

Lights up on the Kitchen, and on BENNO.

BENNO *doesn't change position, but takes part intently in the scene.* MOTHER *and* FATHER *act as though he were present. They talk to him as though he were sitting in the third place set at the table.* BENNO *uses his high voice.*

MOTHER: [*To* FATHER] Eh, Dominick! Where's your old man?
FATHER: How the hell should I know?
MOTHER: He's your father!
[*She busies herself.* FATHER *consults a racing sheet with great interest. He has a pencil in hand and figures numbers along the side of the sheet. After a while, the* MOTHER *glares at him.*]
MOTHER: Look! What is your father, the star boarder? Hanh? Tell me that, what is your father? I tell him and tell him we have supper at six on the dot and does he show? Hanh? Hanh? He don't show. What am I supposed to do with the food—Benno, don't smack your lips like a pig, PIG! Oink, oink, oink—leave it out for the rats? I asked you, Dominick, what am I supposed to do with the food?
[FATHER *ignores her.*]
MOTHER: That's right, Mary, slave for them and let them ignore you. Gotta cook twice, gotta clean up twice, and I work too. What is this, a hotel? Hanh? Your no-good,

free-loadin' father come up to the table afta we finish, like a big rat!

FATHER: Look, fry the steak, I'm hungry. And I want it rare.

MOTHER: Awwww! Eat it raw, you creep!

FATHER: I wanna see the blood. That's how you know it's rare, you can see the blood.

BENNO: [*High voice. Trying to make friends with his* FATHER] That's how you know it's rare, you can see the blood.

MOTHER: [*To* BENNO] You shut up, fatty. What the hell do you know? [*To* FATHER] Looka him bustin' outa those pants and looka those blotches on his face. He's enough to break mirrors, God forbid! And don't get me off the topic of the star boarder. T'resa was sayin' . . .

FATHER: You got red peppers in them potatoes?

MOTHER: We run out.

FATHER: [*Suddenly angry*] God damn it to hell, you know I want red peppers in the fried potatoes! That's when they're good. They burn when they go down.

BENNO: [*As before*] They burn when they go down.

MOTHER: [*To* BENNO] Shut up, you fat creep! [*To* FATHER] And you! Who the hell are you to start screaming at me like you own the place? Hanh? What the hell are you? Nothin', that's what! Up to your ass in debt, a lousy gambler. Who works their ass off? Who slaves? I do—Mary, that's who. I get up and work myself to the bone for you and your monster kid and your free-loading old man. I go to work at six and then have to come home to look after you and this *disgraziato* freak! How much did you give me for the house last week, hanh? Tell me that, big man, big horse player, how much did you give me for the house? A big fat fifteen dollars, that's how much! That's supposed to pay the mortgage, buy food, pay this cripple's doctor bills and keep your no-good, smelly father in stogies! How far's fifteen dollars supposed to go, hanh? What's it supposed to buy— the Taj Mahal? You wanna good meal, you go to the bookie, go to the Pooch! You love him more than you love me!

FATHER: [*Retreating behind the racing form*] All right, all right.

MOTHER: You was always out bettin' them nags. This nag,

this nag, Mary, you never bet on. You want red pepper!
Who the hell are you to want red pepper? You can't
even get it up.

FATHER: You stupid bitch! In front of the kid!

MOTHER: Kid? What kid? Where's the kid? You ever see
a kid that looked like that? He's just like you—nothin'.
A ton of nothin'!

FATHER: [*Angry again*] Whose fault? Hanh? Whose fault?
Without red pepper he can't digest. Red peppers eat
up the fat. You eat red peppers, you can eat anything,
even the shit you cook, and still stay thin and healthy.
The shit you cook! How do you cook it, hanh? By sittin'
on it? It smells of your ass! It smells of your friggin'
cunt!

MOTHER: How would you know? You ain't been in it for
years—all you smell is the Pooch!

FATHER: And another thing, you friggin' Napolitan bitch,
you never, never put enough oregano in the gravy. And
you never put enough oil. It's dry, like your tits! Not
enough red pepper, not enough oregano, not enough
oil, no wonder you got a freak for a son! That's why he
ain't normal!

MOTHER: He ain't normal because he takes after you! He
got no balls either. Your father is ball-less, you is ball-
less. And your kid is ball-less. It runs in the family. I
looked at him last night. There ain't nothin' down
there, only flab. And your father's screwin' a thirteen-
year-old girl. Everybody knows.

FATHER: You shut that big, ugly Napolitan mouth!

MOTHER: *Madonna me'!* The whole neighborhood knows.
Your father's a sex fiend and he's livin' in my house.
And she's a Irish girl, the slut, the *putana!*

FATHER: Shut up! Shut up!

MOTHER: [*Screaming*] Your father's a bum, you're a ball-
less bum with no cock, and your son's a good-for-
nothin' ball-less bum!

FATHER: Cunt!
[*He slaps her. She throws herself to the floor as though
the blow had sent her reeling.*]

BENNO: [*High voice*] Daddy!

MOTHER: [*On the floor, hysterical*] That's right! Run off
to the Pooch! You love him more than you ever loved
me!

BENNO: [*High voice, crying*] Mommy!
MOTHER: Get away from me, you good-for-nothin' fatty,
you! You louse, you good-for-nothin'—you—fruit!
[*Crawls off, weeping.*]
BENNO: My steak is rare, I can see the blood.

BLACKOUT

Scene 5

Lights up on BENNO *and the* GIRL.

The GIRL *is alone. She is dancing to a very ugly, fifties
rock-and-roll tune. She sings along for a moment.* BENNO
stares out, abstracted.

GIRL: Last night I dreamed I was eating a boiled chicken
leg. I started by licking it. I made my tongue all wet
and slobbered all over it, up and down, up and down,
all around. Then, with my front teeth, I tore off the
leg's tip. It was a piece of skin, yellow. I rolled the skin
under my teeth, sucking all the juice out of it. Then, I
spit it out. Then, suddenly, I stuck all my teeth into the
middle of the leg and let it dangle in my mouth. Not
biting, not chewing, just letting it dangle.
[*She freezes in place. The light on her dims but does
not go out. A tape of the ugly rock tune is heard. On
the tape, the* GIRL *is singing very softly into a closely
held microphone. The sound is breathy and wet. Then
the tape fades very slowly under the following.*]
BENNO: [*He starts slowly, with little expression.*] Benno
loved to draw. And he loved drawings. As soon as he
was old enough he stole carfare from his mother's purse
and went to the big museum. He snuck in. He ran to
the Renaissance paintings. And he stared at them. He
stared at their designs, most particularly at their designs. And at their colors. But the designs, to begin
with, were the most significant to him. The circle, for
instance, fascinated him; and the right angle as used in
a painting like *The Last Supper* thrilled him. He would

trace the angles and the circles in these paintings with his fingers when the guards weren't looking. Then, on paper napkins and the dirty lined paper from the Catholic school, he would make designs like those. He drew arcs and circles, and angles and lines, trying to vary them with the deception and subtlety of the masters. He wasn't interested in drawing people. He knew what they looked like. Think of the structure of the foot. The lines bend, then they curve. The arch juts up, then juts down; two angles, like a roof. Underneath there is the inverse. The sole is like a barreled vault. Then, at the front, five straight lines—but with rounded tips. Benno drew idealized feet, or distorted them in his own way. He was not interested in the imperfections of real feet. Benno's make-believe feet were curved or gracefully inclined. Real feet are crooked and crushed. One day, out of guilt, Benno's Pop-pop bought him a paint set with a Social Security check that bounced or something and caused some discomfort. Benno painted—he colored in his designs. He painted hour upon hour upon hour. He lulled himself asleep planning paintings as though they were battle campaigns. He dreamed colored designs and designs of colors and waking, tried to copy these. Once, once when he had finished painting six straight lines carefully, he stared at his painting and heard . . . heard music played up the back of his spine. It made no difference. When he had finished a painting, Benno was still fat, ugly, and alone. Nothing makes a difference, nothing alters anything. It took Benno a very long time to learn this. And Benno wasn't sure he had learned it, really, until he started eating himself to death. Then Benno knew he had learned. For all that matters is the taste of our own flesh. It tastes horrible, particularly if we are fat and sweat a lot. But there are no disappointments there; and those feelings of horror and disgust at chewing ourselves are the only feelings we can be sure of. Benno will put his eyes out soon. Then there will be no seductive angles or circles. Benno will be left to stumble about his filthy room, the windows nailed shut, biting at himself. Thank you.

[*The lights go out on* BENNO. *They intensify on the* GIRL, *who starts singing and dancing again.*]

GIRL: So anyway, then I dreamed that I tore off the bite

in my mouth. Just then I was woke up by my brother screaming. He sleeps in the bed next to mine. His underpants were covered in jit. He'd had a wet dream. [*She sniggers.*] He didn't know what it was. I did. I didn't tell him what it was. He started crying. He thought he was gonna die. I let him think so. I'm hungry. I hope Mom serves chicken soon.

BLACKOUT

Scene 6

The lights come up on BENNO *and on the Park.*

The GIRL *and* OLD MAN *are lying down. The light is heavy and shadowy.*

OLD MAN: [*Looks off, nervous.*] Damn kids! Make a lotta noise. Benno, why you no play wit them?

BENNO: [*High voice*] What, Pop-pop?

OLD MAN: Why you no have friends, Benno? Why you always around me?

BENNO: [*High voice*] I love you, Pop-pop.

[*The* GIRL *laughs, mocking.*]

BENNO: I do love you, Pop-pop.

OLD MAN: [*To* BENNO] Shut up, you crazy, you. If you gonna stay around be quiet. Stay over there.

BENNO: [*High voice*] I'm drawing, Pop-pop. I'll be quiet.

[*The* OLD MAN *draws closer to the* GIRL *and whispers in her ear.*]

OLD MAN: You very pretty for an Irish girl. I like you hair, it is so long and thick. And you thighs, they very soft. When I touch them, I feel them long time after.

GIRL: You have bumps on your feet. And there's somethin' strange on your heels. It's like moss.

OLD MAN: You fingers is beautiful. You toes is beautiful. [*Sucks on her fingers.*]

BENNO: [*High voice*] Pop-pop . . .

OLD MAN: [*Very annoyed*] Benno, go 'way! I'm tellin' you,

go 'way. Go over to them boys in the trees over there.
Go play wit them. You hear me, Benno? Go on!
[*Gets up and mimes chasing* BENNO *away.* BENNO
reacts facially in place. The OLD MAN, *looking off as
though following* BENNO *with his eyes.*]
OLD MAN: Maybe they be friends for him.
GIRL: Benno's so fat.
OLD MAN: He's my oldest grandchild.
GIRL: He's a monster. Ooooo! He's so ugly. Benno Blim-
pie, we call him.
OLD MAN: Lemme get on top a you.
GIRL: No, use your fingers like you did yesterday.
OLD MAN: I wanna do somethin' different.
GIRL: Somethin' different? [*Caresses his thigh.*] What? I
don't wanna do nothin' different. [*Sticks her tongue in
his mouth.*]
OLD MAN: I gotta do somethin' different.
GIRL: What?
OLD MAN: Somethin'. You like it.
GIRL: What'll you give me?
OLD MAN: My Social Security check comes next week. I
give you if you let me.
GIRL: How much?
OLD MAN: Sixty-two twenty.
GIRL: Bring it next week. We'll see then. Use your fingers
today.
OLD MAN: [*Reaches under her dress.*] Like this?
GIRL: [*Spreads her legs.*] Yes.
OLD MAN: Touch me.
[*The* GIRL *starts to unzip him.* BENNO *screams.*]
OLD MAN: Damn it to hell! That's Benno.
[*They both look off and the* OLD MAN *rises.*]
GIRL: It's them boys. They got him.
OLD MAN: Shit! [*Starts to go off.*]
GIRL: [*Holds him back.*] Don't go. They're just playin'.
That's how boys play nowadays. Come on. Use your
fingers today. Next week bring me the check. Kiss me.
OLD MAN: Like this? [*Kisses her.*]
GIRL: Use your fingers.
OLD MAN: [*Reaches under her dress*] Like this?
GIRL: [*Unzipping him*] Yes . . . yes . . .
BENNO: [*Screaming as though terrified and in pain*] Pop-
pop! Pop-pop! Pop-pop!

[*Blackout.* BENNO *continues screaming for a beat in the dark. Then silence.*]

Scene 7

Lights up on the Kitchen and on BENNO.

FATHER *hovers about the stove.*

FATHER: Goddammit, Benno, quit followin' me. Where did she keep things, Benno? You know where that bitch, God forgive me, kept everything? Aw—how would you know? Sit down. How many eggs you want, Benno? Six enough? Benno, I make seven, that should fill us both. I hope she dies in that filthy Napolitan shack livin' with her virgin sister. Get the black pepper, Benno—don't spill it—watch out, don't spill it. Be careful, or you'll spill it; watch out . . . shit fire, you spilled it! Why are you so clumsy, my son? [*Stoops down as though picking black pepper up off the floor.*] Hey! I know what. I'll put pepperoni in the eggs. That's always good! [*Sings as he mimes adding the ingredients.*] "Pepperoni hits the spot, helps you shit because it's hot." Why didn't you fight back, Benno, hanh? Why didn't you fight back? I heard, I heard, Benno, what them kids did to you. Why did you lay there like some queer? Hanh! I'll turn the heat up just a tidge: And maybe we better put some milk. Is there somethin' wrong with you, my son? Are you a pansy, my son? Why ain't you out there in the street, playin' ball, roughin' up like I did? Why you always in here with you mama, like a girl? Shit, the eggs is stickin' to the pan, I'll stir them. We better put a tidge of sugar in. There. Why are you so fat, my son? Why don't you exercise? I'd never of let them kids near me when I was your age. I'll put some oregano in. Never. I'll tell you, I was a holy terror, a holy terror, geez. I'd have kicked them inna balls, like this. I'd have beat them with my fists, like this. I was no fatty, no pansy. I'd have punched them, I'd have beaten them senseless.

[*Dances around as though in a boxing ring.*] Left, right, left, right and kick to the balls. [*Mimes a fight.*] Take that, motherfucker, take that and that! A right to the side of the head—pow! A left to the jaw and boop!—a knee between the legs! And another left and another right—he's down, he's bleedin'—my God!—he's out! Hey! Hey! [*Runs to the stove.*] Shit! Shit fire and save the matches! The eggs is burned.

BLACKOUT

Scene 8

Lights up on BENNO *and on the* GIRL. *Near her is a small night table with stained and sticky-looking bottles and jars on it.*

When the light hits her she sprays a large amount of very smelly hair spray on her hair, then teases her hair violently. Then she smears an enormous amount of purple lipstick on sensuously puffed-out lips. During this she sings a very ugly rock tune and occasionally does a dance step to it.

GIRL: Last night I spilled spaghetti all over me. The sauce went over my white blouse and my blue dress; and it was thick sauce with peppers and bits of meat in it. It was a big mess. And Donny, my cousin, wiped it off. He's spiffy. Twenty and in the Navy. He took his napkin, it had red stains from his mouth on it, and wiped my blouse off. Wiped and wiped, not too hard but strong. Then he took another napkin, my brother's, and wiped my dress off. Wiped and wiped, makin' a small circle in my lap. Donny has big hands, a lotta hair on them around the knuckles and the veins is very thick. His fingers is thick, too, and the middle one is long and heavy. I dream about Donny's hand makin' circles in my lap.
[*Freezes in place. The light on her dims.*]

BENNO: Benno grew up thinking that talent and sensitivity were things people took seriously. At least that important people took seriously—artists, for instance, and teachers. Benno grew up hoping that looks and sex didn't matter. That paintings would satisfy any longing he'd ever have. And when that longing got too strong, a quick pulling with the palm would be enough. Benno was wrong. Benno has been heard to say that nothing matters save the taste of his own flesh. But since then, time has passed. For your benefit he has conjured up scenes better not remembered. And Benno realizes that he was guilty of oversimplification. There are things that matter: looks matter, sex matters. These are all that matter. Benno feels that those who deny this are participating in a huge joke. Benno has learned his lesson. Paintings, you see, aren't enough. When loneliness and emptiness and longing congeal like a jelly, nothing assuages the ache. Nothing, nothing, nothing. It was the end of spring, the traditional season of youth, renewal, and young love. Benno returned to his old neighborhood, having celebrated his twentieth birthday. He found the poorest side street in his old neighborhood. Fitzgerald Street, by name. And he rented a room on the third floor of a row house on Fitzgerald Street. Benno nailed shut all the windows in that room, even though it was summer. Something about imbibing his own smell. Benno is not as isolated as you might think. He hears the horrible street noises. He hears the monster children screaming. He even allows himself to have his shade up one-half hour a day. Today at 1 P.M., Benno had his shade up. He stared out his nailed window, stared through the caked dirt that streaks the window's glass. He saw a wild circle flashing red across the street. He stared at that circle and was tempted to . . . never mind. He was tempted and stared and was tempted some more. And then he saw the agent of that circle. It was a little girl. A beautiful girl. Oh yes, Benno knows beauty. He knows if he tell you. Once, when he saw something beautiful, it would flash across his eyes like a hot knife and he would peer, eyes stuck there until they ached. Once, he tells you, no longer. For beauty has lost his power over me, it has lost its power, no more beauty, no more longing to grasp it within me and smother it with my bulk, please God, no more beauty. [*He is almost weeping. He eats passionately and slowly pulls himself together.*]

GIRL: [*Unfreezes and continues with her makeup.*] When Donny finished wiping me off, I smiled up at him and his eyes, they're black, got very big. When Ma wasn't looking, I let my fingers take a walk along his thigh. I saw the big bump in the middle of his thigh get bigger. Then, when Ma was clearin' the table, I spilled the plate of meatballs all over me. While she was in the kitchen, Donny licked them off with his tongue. Ma caught him and gave him hell. Pop laughed. Donny ran into the bathroom and puked all over, like a sissy. I changed my mind about Donny. I think Donny is a jerk-off.

[*Lights out on* GIRL.]

BENNO: Benno has decided: he will no longer lift the shade, he will no longer look out into the street. Benno stayed in this tiny room. He left every two days to buy food. Otherwise he never went out. Except in cases of emergency such as when the ice cream truck came along. He did nothing. He ate continually from when he awoke until he fell asleep. He did nothing save remember. When I become so fat I cannot get into his clothes and can barely move, I will nail the door shut. I will put his eyes out with a long nail and I will bite at himself until he dies. In the middle of this filthy hole on the third floor of a row house in the poorest side street of my old neighborhood there will I be: a mountain of flesh. There are rats in this room. I see them slithering along the sides of the wall. They will eat me. These rats will find Benno beautiful. They will long for him. He will be a sexual object to them. They will make the devouring of Benno's body an erotic act. They will gnaw hollows into his face, into his belly. And in those hollows, they will fornicate. Then they will perish. The instant before he is ready to die, Benno will swallow a hugh draft of poison. These rats in eating Benno will be eating poisoned meat. The poison will cause a fearful splitting of stomachs, vital rat organs will swell up and burst even while the rats are making

love. Even while they are eating. Posthumously, Benno
will have been loved.

BLACKOUT

Scene 9

Lights up on Park and on BENNO.

The GIRL *and the* OLD MAN *are seated together on the
ground. The* OLD MAN *has a wine bottle in a paper bag
with him and takes swigs from it. The* GIRL *is in a Catholic schoolgirl's uniform—white blouse; blue, rather long
skirt; and white ankle socks with blue oxfords. She has
a school satchel nearby.*

OLD MAN: Benno, you stay over there and draw. Don'
bother me. You old enough to go pee-pee by yourself.
GIRL: He's funny, retarded.
OLD MAN: You hear me, Benno?
BENNO: [*High voice*] Yes, Pop-pop.
GIRL: [*Mimicking*] Yes, Pop-pop.
OLD MAN: Just be sure you stay away! An' don' you go
tellin' you bitch mother, either.
.BENNO: [*High voice*] I won't, Pop-pop.
GIRL: Queerie!
OLD MAN: You hear me good, Benno. Leave me alone
today.
BENNO: [*High voice*] Yes, Pop-pop. [*Quietly to himself,
high voice*] I love you, Pop-pop. [*Normal voice, to the
audience*] And Benno wept. He didn't realize at that
time that there is nothing funnier than a fat boy weep-
ing. Nothing funnier. Nothing. [*A pause. He laughs
dryly. The light dims somewhat on* BENNO. *But he
stares at the scene intently.*]
OLD MAN: [*Takes a drink, offers the bottle to the* GIRL.]
Drink this!
GIRL: Don' wan' none.
OLD MAN: Drink.

GIRL: Don' wan' none, I said! [*Takes a long swig and grimaces.*] Oooooooh! What is it?

OLD MAN: *La vita, carina, la vita.*

GIRL: Don' know Eyetalian. You bring the check?

OLD MAN: Sixty-two twenty.

GIRL: Lemme see.

OLD MAN: Later.

GIRL: Lemme see.

[*He reaches into his back pocket and presents her with the check. She scrutinizes it.*]

GIRL: Yeah . . . yeah . . . sixty-two twenty. Sign it over to me.

OLD MAN: What do you mean?

GIRL: You know what I mean. Sign it over.

OLD MAN: Can't write.

GIRL: Make yer sign.

OLD MAN: Got no pencil.

GIRL: Got one in my school bag. [*Reaches into her school bag and removes a pencil.*] New point. Come on.

OLD MAN: All right.

[*Makes his mark on the check. The* GIRL *reaches for the wine and takes a long pull.*]

GIRL: [*As he notices her drinking*] Didn't have no lunch today. On a diet. Give it to me.

OLD MAN: Afta. [*Puts check in his back pocket.*]

GIRL: Benno hangs around you a lot. Why? He ain't normal.

OLD MAN: Kiss me.

GIRL: My brother beat him up, broke his glasses. Said he wanted to crush his nose against his face like a pimple.

OLD MAN: Touch me.

GIRL: You love Benno?

OLD MAN: Let me do it now, I be gentle.

GIRL: Do you love him?

OLD MAN: I take you top off.

GIRL: [*Twists away.*] Yesterday my brother told me he gonna beat Benno up afta school on Monday. You gonna try and stop him?

OLD MAN: Help me wit you buttons.

GIRL: Not yet. Use your fingers.

OLD MAN: Want more today. Help me wit the buttons.

GIRL: [*He tries to start undressing the* GIRL. *She resists,*

but in a lazy, teasing way. The OLD MAN *sometimes
stops trying to remove her top and caresses her.*] Why
is Benno so weird? Drawing all the time. Never playin'
in the street? In school on Tuesday—c'mon, cut it out—
he started talkin' about this Eyetalian painter. Just
started talking; sister didn't call on him or nothing. Cut
that out. Then Benno showed us his drawings. They
was weird. One was supposed to be a old man. He was
long and thin with these blurry features. Looked like
my brother's dickie floatin' in the bathtub. Stop it! I
don't like you slobbering on me!

OLD MAN: Drink some more. [*Takes a long swig and
passes her the bottle.*]

GIRL: Lick my feet like you did before. [*Drinks.*]

OLD MAN: I want more—I want more. [*Gets on top of
her.*]

BENNO: [*High voice, loudly*] Pop-pop, look what I drew.
Look, see the circles. . . .

OLD MAN: [*Jumping off the* GIRL] God damn it to hell,
Benno! Get away from here, go on! [*Acts as though
chasing* BENNO *off.*] Damn kid, always around, always
in the way. [*Lies down beside the* GIRL.]

GIRL: [*Giggles.*] Benno couldn't genuflect at mass on
Wednesday. He couldn't get that far down. And when
he did get down on his knees, he couldn't get up. Even
sister laughed. Then we all had to go to confession for
laughing at mass. Even sister. I smelled the priest in
the confessional. All sweaty and underarmy. But nice.
Do you love Benno?

OLD MAN: [*Caressing her, kissing her hair*] You, *carina*,
you I love; all of you. Fine Irish hair and the little hairs
down there. I wanna scoop you up with my mouth. You
hear me, with my mouth! I wanna bury my teeth, bury
them, in there, in and in and in. Come to me, *cara*, I
ready. I wan' . . .

GIRL: [*Squirming away*] You wanna, you wanna, you
wanna! You're drunk, you're a slob!

OLD MAN: I wan' more from you this time, this time more!

GIRL: Hey, hey!

[*He reaches under her dress.*]

GIRL: I'm not in the mood! [*She reaches for the bottle
and takes a long swig.*]

OLD MAN: [*Lies back and strokes her.*] In the *paese*, over there, over the seas, I took a little girl inna wood. I was how old? Nineteen maybe, who knows? I take her inna the wood and swallow her whole. You hear, swallow her whole?! I start at her feet. [*Grabs the* GIRL's *foot. She utters an annoyed cry.*] Took her toes inna my mouth and bite them off, one by one. Then I bite inna her leg . . . [*Grabs her leg and holds it tight while she struggles.*] . . . and chew onna the bone. It was hard that bone, but then, then I have good teeth and chew hard. I ate all of her, and today, today I wan' more. . . . [*The* GIRL *finally pushes him away with all her strength.*]

GIRL: No! I'm sick of you and your yellow skin and your sores and your smell!

OLD MAN: [*Trying to get on top of her*] Bella mia, mia bella, ti voglio! I wanna dig inna you skin!

GIRL: [*Twisting away*] Dago shit! Smelly!

BENNO: [*High voice*] Pop-pop! Pop-pop!

[*The* OLD MAN *has begun to chase the* GIRL, *reaching out for her. This has started slowly but becomes wild. The* OLD MAN *starts gasping for breath and getting dizzy.*]

BENNO: [*High voice*] Why are you running like that, Pop-pop? Stop it, I'm scared!

GIRL: [*Dodging the* OLD MAN *as though it were a game*] Grandson's a queerie, granddad's a smelly!

OLD MAN: [*Still chasing her, panting*] I wan' more, more!

BENNO: [*High voice*] Please, Pop-pop!

GIRL: Smelly!

BENNO: [*High voice*] Leave her alone, Pop-pop!

OLD MAN: [*Gasping*] Mia! Bella mia, ti voglio! Fermati! T'amo!

GIRL: Wop bastard!

[*The* OLD MAN *lunges and catches the* GIRL. *She utters a cry and fights him. Neither is playful. The* OLD MAN *throws her to the ground. She screams. He tries to hurl himself on top of her but she moves at the last minute and he hits the ground with a thud and a cry. He is stunned briefly.*]

BENNO: [*High voice*] Oh! Oh, Pop-pop . . .

[*The* GIRL *runs to the wine bottle and breaks it.*]

GIRL: [*Waving the broken bottle*] Come on, dago shit, come on!

OLD MAN: [*Laughs.*] *Tigra, tigra,* come on, *tigra!*
[*They circle each other slowly. Occasionally the* GIRL
strikes out at the OLD MAN. *He is playful but she is
very serious. From his stool* BENNO *watches in terror.*]
BENNO: Pop-pop, should I run for the police?
OLD MAN: [*To the* GIRL, *still circling*] I wanna chew you
up!
GIRL: Asshole! [*Lunges again and cuts him on the arm.*]
OLD MAN: [*Yells but chases her more violently.*] Mia,
vieni!
BENNO: Leave her alone, Pop-pop, she's crazy!
[*The* OLD MAN *acts as though* BENNO *is tugging at him
and turns to push him away.*]
OLD MAN: Go home, queerie, go home! Today I wan'
more. . . .
[*With a scream the* GIRL *lunges and stabs the* OLD MAN
*in the back with the broken bottle. He screams and
falls.*]
OLD MAN: [*Screaming*] Aiuto, aiuto, Benno, help me!
[*He twists desperately in the mud as though trying to
stop the pain in his back.* BENNO *gasps, then stares.
The* GIRL *also stares wide-eyed. The* OLD MAN *continues to scream and throws up in the mud.*]
GIRL: [*In a stunned whisper*] Go 'head, puke, you wop
bastard!
OLD MAN: [*Almost voiceless*] I . . . I . . . I . . .
[*Dies. There is a pause. The* GIRL *becomes suddenly
hysterical.*]
GIRL: Bastard! Bastard! Filthy wop bastard! Oh, my God,
my God, I've . . . I've . . . he's . . . [*With a cry she
throws the bottle down. It shatters. She looks at it
frightened, then bends over the corpse, screaming.*]
Dago, dago, wop, filthy, dago bastard, bastard, bitch,
dago, jerk-off, bitch, motherfucker, filthy . . . mother
. . . [*She is gasping. She pulls herself together suddenly
and looks around.*] Geez . . . the check! [*She searches
the body for the check and finds it. She removes it
from the back pocket.*] Muddy. [*Wipes the check on
her skirt.*] Hey . . . hey . . . you kiddin'? [*Kicks the
body.*] Oh . . . oh, Caarist! Hey, Benno, your Pop-pop's
dead. Don't you tell nobody or my brother'll get you
good. Oh'. . . [*Looks at the body.*] Oh . . . Caarist! [*Runs
off.*]

BENNO: [*A pause. Then he whispers, normal voice*] Pop-pop.

BLACKOUT

Scene 10

Lights up on BENNO *and the Kitchen. The* FATHER *is pacing tensely.*

FATHER: Where the hell is your mother, Benno? Hanh? Mary! Mary! Where the hell are you! We should be there! Mary!

MOTHER: [*Offstage*] All right, for Christ's sake, I'm comin'!

FATHER; Jesus Christ—let me make sure everythin' is ready, Benno. [*Opens ice box.*] Yep, got the spareribs for the gravy—Uncle Fonse likes them—Benno—don't eat the cake, it's for the relatives, afta. [*Calling*] Mary, for Christ's sake, hurry.

MOTHER: [*Off*] Jesus Christ in heaven shove that friggin' racin' form in that big mouth, I'm comin'!

[*A pause. She enters. She seems ashamed. The dress she is wearing is too small for her. He looks at her.*]

FATHER: Jesus—is that all you had to wear?

MOTHER: Ain't had no money to buy a dress in years—

FATHER: Well, at least they'll know you was Benno's mother and you eat well—wear a shawl or somethin'. Come on.

MOTHER: Not yet.

FATHER: Oh, Jesus!

MOTHER: I ain't ready yet! Gotta get inna the mood. I don't like wakes. You go on, I'll come later. Not ready, I tell you.

FATHER: And the kid?

MOTHER: Why can't you take him, you ashamed? You think they'll think he's my fault if he comes in wit me? Hanh? Is that what you think? Oh, their little Dominick could never commit somethin' like this flabby monster.

He could never cause such ugliness to come inna the world. It's Mary's fault.

FATHER: Look you, none of your shit tonight. You keep that big ugly Napolitan mouth shut. And you bring the kid. It's my father's wake and I want you to show some respect, or so help me God, I'll take the strap to you right there.

MOTHER: All right, all right, get the hell out.

FATHER: Make sure that kid keeps decent too. [*Exits.*]

MOTHER: Let's have some coffee, Benno. I need it. [*Heats coffee.*] Oh, Jesus, Jesus, how'm I gonna face it? All them relatives of his: his sister Edith, that witch of a prune face, *faccia brutt', Virgine, ti conosci'*, Benno stop slobberin', and his brother, Basil—face like a rhinoceros' ass—how'm I gonna face them? They hate me. They look down on me—Mary the peasant, they call me. But it was me, the Virgin knows, me, Mary the horse, put the old man up. Me! I hadda see him come and spit inna the sink every day. Me! And I hadda run the vacuum cleaner to get the scales from his sores. Those damn scales were everywhere, like fairy dust. I even found 'em on the windowsill. How did they get on the windowsill? What did he do, scratch them while watchin' some broad walk down the street? And do they thank me for cleanin' up afta him week afta friggin' week? Nah! Benno, why you puttin' five teaspoons of sugar in you coffee, hanh? Why can't you put two like a human being? Three, even three I could see, God knows, but five? Who do you take afta? Hanh? [*Gets up and pours coffee for herself.*] Take some coffee, Mary. Weep into them grounds. And them goddamned lousy shits look down at me. My father, my friggin' father, God rest his soul, was eight times, nah, nine times the man theirs was! Nine times, you hear me? The day before he died I went a see him. Couldn't find him. Where was he, where? Then, suddenly, I hear this clang, this loud clang. CLANG! It come from the cellar. I run down. There he is, seventy-six, at least, chasin' rats with the shovel. He screamed: *Ecco! Ecco!* And then he smashes one with the shovel. CLANG!! It splattered all over the cellar. That was a real man. Not a ball-less bum like you no-good bastard father. Well, have a cookie, Mary, you deserve it. [*To* BENNO] No

more for you, dinosaur, you've had seven. No more, I
said. You shit, you!
[*Pantomimes reaching over and slapping his hand.*
BENNO *winces in place, as though fighting back tears.*]
MOTHER: Cry baby! Looka him hold back the tears. No-
good sissy! Men don't cry. And looka! Just a big lump
of lard. Jesus, I could store you up and cook with you.
What did I do, oh Virgin, to deserve all this suffering?
Hanh? Looka them pimples. Don't scratch them you
no-good! If only you wasn't so flabby. If only you had
some muscle on them monster arms and legs. But all
you is is a huge, flabby rat. You hear me? A rat; with
them big, black dartin' eyes. I'm sick a you; and sick
a that creep you no-good bastard father. Who goes out
and works like a dog? Me! Who comes home and cleans
like a horse? Hanh? I do! And who put that no-good
bum, your Pop-pop, God rest his soul, up for years and
years and then he has to go out and let some nigger
stab him with his own wine bottle and we don't even
get his last check, god damn it all to hell, *I* did and *I*
do, that's who! Mary! Mary the horse! Mary the horse,
they call me—don't take another cookie, you pig—Mary
the horse. [*She is becoming hysterical.*] They used a
call me Bella, beautiful, you know that? Beautiful and
I had red hair, flaming, and big boobs, almost as big as
yours, you little queer, and a shape, *Madone'*, what a
shape! Old Joey Fercanti, I coulda married him, said
my lips should be on the silver screen, that's how big
they were and thick and red. Bella, Bella they called
me. And when I danced they look at me, and when I
walked home from the market even with a dozen other
girls, they looked at me, and when I got married all the
guys in the neighborhood got drunk. Bella! And look
at me now—I'm almost as ugly as you, I'm a hag, a
bitch! Got no shape no more and my hair's gray and
fallin' out and your father, your father that no-good
lousy son of a bitch did this to me, worked at me and
worked at me, a rat, chewin' at me, with big dartin'
eyes and tearin' me to pieces! Look at me good. Oh,
my God, my God, how did I wind up like this, with the
peelin' wallpaper and nothin' else, no furniture, no
money, not a decent dress. What am I gonna wear to
that wake? They'll laugh, you hear me, they'll laugh.

[*She has reached a frenzy. And sobs for a moment and then slowly begins to calm down. Occasionally her chest heaves from sobbing.* BENNO *stares wide-eyed. She has calmed down. Slowly she rises and pours herself another cup of coffee.*]

MOTHER: Have some more coffee, Mary. That's all you got, caffeine, that's all you got in the whole world. [*To* BENNO] And you, monster, you with them big eyes, them big black eyes, what do you want now?

BENNO: [*High voice, soft*] A cookie.

[MOTHER *sobs. Lights dim on* MOTHER.]

Scene 11

BENNO *speaks urgently to the audience.*

BENNO: And what about love? Specifically, what about sexual love? Did or did not this fat one ever have congress with anything other than his palm? Benno wonders: should he describe his sexual past? Benno is ravenous for himself and time it presses on. Benno must cease this night or face yet one other two-day cycle.

[*Out of the shadows comes the* OLD MAN. *He is dressed in a long butcher's apron. It is abnormally white and quite long. The* OLD MAN's *hair has been whitened and so has his face. There is a golden aura about him so that even though he is recognizably a butcher, there is something angelic in his appearance as well. He carries a golden meat cleaver and a black crayon. During the following, as* BENNO *speaks, the* OLD MAN *pulls over his head an enormous white robe. When the robe is fully on* BENNO, *the* OLD MAN *prepares to draw on it with his crayon. He will draw on* BENNO *a butcher's chart identifying the various slices of meat.* BENNO *submits to all this without paying any attention.* BENNO *speaks laconically and with a certain irony. The lights on him becomes brighter and brighter as he speaks.*]

BENNO: Benno and sex: a story. Benno went out one night. He was fourteen. His Pop-pop had been dead—

how many years? They blur too much for Benno to know for sure. Had Benno been an intellectual he would have concerned himself with the nature of time. Benno felt that the secret of time was perhaps his secret. Maybe Benno was the product of a time warp. Benno then would have been the bloated issue of an inverted time womb which, due to God-joke, or cosmic spasm, vomited him out long before, or long after, his true time. But when, he asks you, when would have been Benno's time? Some of us, it seems, exist outside of nature and no one knows where we fit. Nature has her claws in all of you but not in we who exist outside her. You have your claws in us. I see that you all think Benno speaks nonsense. My mouth is dry. Perhaps what he says to you, even to the very words, is unfamiliar. Perhaps it is Hungarian he speaks or some curious combination of frothy diphthongs. Benno always had a problem with his saliva.

[*Out of the dark come the voices of* FATHER *and* MOTHER.]

MOTHER'S VOICE: Not only a fatty, but he drools, too. Looka that: it's like a broken water fountain!

FATHER'S VOICE: Is there something wrong with you, my son?

BENNO: Benno ran out one night. In the best tradition of arts and letters there beat in him the age-old desperation. Benno felt those horrible waves of longing wash over him and tumble back on himself and he could do nothing about it. There was no cure for that longing in Benno. No church socials sponsored his dreams of satiety; no youth organization provided him with a concourse to fulfillment; and double dating was out. There was no cure out of popular sentiment, nor out of clinical misassessment. Benno was singular and had to suffer alone. Sometimes I want to run to my nailed windows and vomit out them. The force, the force of my vomit, would explode through the window onto the passersby and crush them. And crush them.

[*He pauses for a moment. The* OLD MAN *is now ready to draw on him.*]

BENNO: Benno Blimpie: The sensuous fatso. Prefatory to his supper of self.

OLD MAN: Breast! [*Draws the lines around* BENNO'S

breasts, as a butcher's chart would show them, and labels them.]
BENNO: The fourteen-year-old Benno ran out one night . . .
OLD MAN: Rib! [*As before, draws the lines and labels them.*]
BENNO: Benno was looking for love.
OLD MAN: Chuck! [*As before, draws and labels lines.*]
BENNO: Benno was looking for love!
MOTHER'S VOICE: [*Off. In the dark*] You think we should put him away?
FATHER'S VOICE: Who?
MOTHER'S VOICE: Who else? Our humpback of Notre Dame son!
BENNO: For love.
OLD MAN: Round. [*As before, draws on* BENNO *and labels him.*]
BENNO: Benno took a walk. He ended up in Edgar Allan Poe schoolyard. A place of concrete, broken glass, and dog shit. Dried dog shit of the peculiarly urban sort. In the schoolyard, Benno saw three boys. They lounged about in the shadows, some distance from him. They were older than Benno, from his neighborhood. He saw the schoolyard to be a place of waste; to be a locus of the city's fecal matter. Yes, he saw that broken glass, that concrete with the brown grass jutting, and that hard dog shit to be part of a gigantic fecal mass; yes, and he saw those boys with their T-shirts and torn dungarees also as so many turds. Nor was Benno himself exempt; he too was waste. All was waste. Waste. Through the haze of this decay, Benno saw these boys, and chose to wait.
OLD MAN: Sirloin . . . [*As before, draws, then labels.*]
BENNO: In due course, the boys noticed Benno. They performed the usual ritual of greeting Benno. They pointed and giggled.
OLD MAN: Rump. [*As before, draws, then labels.*]
BENNO: Hey, kid, one said, hey, kid. They beckoned me closer. I went. What you name, kid, they asked. They knew already. Benno, he replied. Hey, they sang out, Benno Blimpie. Hey, fellas, meet Benno Blimpie.
OLD MAN: Loin. [*Draws and labels, as before.*]
BENNO: The tallest said: Hey, Benno, know what this is?

He grabbed his crotch. My mouth was dry. Yes, Benno was heard to whisper, I know. They laughed. Hey, fellas, they sang out, Benno Blimpie knows.

OLD MAN: Liver. [*Draws and labels* BENNO.]

BENNO: The oldest lowered his voice and said: Hey, Benno, you wanna eat me?

OLD MAN: Kidney. [*Draws and labels* BENNO.]

BENNO: I said nothing. Sure he does, one said. Benno wants to eat us all. The oldest said: Sure, Benno wants a big meal, he wants to eat us all. They settled the order, one taking watch, one watching me, the other being served. They pushed me down, it took all three. And one after the other I ate them. I ate all three.

OLD MAN: Heart. [*Labels and draws on* BENNO.]

BENNO: I ate all three. One, two, and three. I caught on after a bit. They were happy during it and pranced around. They enjoyed it. When Benno had finished all three, they bloodied his nose and forced one eye shut by pounding it. Then they picked up pieces of glass and dried dog shit and stuffed them into Benno's bleeding mouth. Laughing, they ran off. I was left lying like a blimp in the middle of the public schoolyard. In the middle of all that concrete, with come and shit and glass in my mouth. I couldn't cry; Benno couldn't scream. He lay there; and in that instant, time stopped. And feeling, it stopped too, and seemed to merge with time, and with space. My sense of identity seeped out of me into the cracks in the concrete. And for a few seconds I was out of myself, totally free of myself. Totally. Free. Free. And this I call: The Transfiguration of Benno Blimpie.

Scene 12

Lights come up intensely on everyone. The OLD MAN *hands* BENNO *the meat cleaver.*

OLD MAN: You ready now!

[*Slowly,* BENNO *rises from his chair with great effort.*

He raises the meat cleaver. Everyone turns and watches him in silence.]

BENNO: I am Benno. I am eating myself to death.

[*Slowly he lowers the meat cleaver as though to cut off some part of himself. The others watch intently. As he reaches that part, quick blackout.*]